Patricia O'Reilly

DYING WITH LOVE

VERITAS

First published 1992 by
Veritas Publications
7-8 Lower Abbey Street
Dublin 1

1 2 3 4 5

Copyright © Patricia O'Reilly 1992

ISBN 1 85390 139 3

**British Library Cataloguing
in Publication Data.
A catalogue record for
this book is available
from the British Library.**

Cover design by creative a.d., Dublin
Cover photograph by Don Sutton
Printed in the Republic of Ireland
by the Leinster Leader

This book is dedicated to all those who made it possible by allowing me to become part of their life and death.

THANKS TO THE FOLLOWING

Dr Michael Kearney, Our Lady's Hospice
Sr Ignatius, Our Lady's Hospice
Dr Veronie Hanly, Our Lady's Hospice
Sr Francis Rose, Our Lady's Hospice
Térèse Brady, Department of Psychology, UCD,
  and Irish Hospice Foundation
Dr Andrew McGrady
Mary Killeen, St Vincent's Hospital
Dr Esther Bradley
Dr Michael Fitzgerald, psychoanalyst and child
  psychiatrist
Dr Sheila McGauran
Beatrice Doran, Royal College of Surgeons
Dublin Samaritans
ISIDA (Irish Sudden Infant Death Association)
Coping
Marian Greene, Eastern Health Board,
  Community Care
Larry Massey Funeral Services, Dublin
Gerry Griffin & Sons Funeral Home, Limerick
George McCullough, Glasnevin Crematorium
  Company Ltd
SunLife of Canada
Irish Insurance Federation

While the case histories described in this book are based on fact, names, locations and circumstances have been altered to preserve anonymity.

Contents

PREFACE

This is a book about people and about hope. It is my hope that in some small way *Dying with Love* will bring acceptance and peace into the lives of those who read it and that it will help to change our modern attitude to death, which has become one of the taboos of this century. Most of us are quite happy to talk about birth and living, but too often we shun any discussion of dying and death.

To research and write this book, I had to accept and, indeed, become comfortable with my own mortality and, because living and dying are so inextricably bound up, I was also forced to take stock of my own life. It was a cathartic experience. I emerged from it believing surely that dying – that last hurdle of living – is the ultimate act of love.

I watched and listened and was moved by those who were dying and their carers. Their common attributes were their acceptance of death, strength of spirit and indomitable courage. Somewhere along the line, I became unshackled from my own fear of dying and since then my own living has been all the sweeter.

If given the choice most people would prefer to spend the last days of their life at home, but currently more than half of our population dies in hospital. With the improvements in modern drugs, and with palliative care and Hospice home care teams, the majority of people can die at home; nobody need die in pain and it is everyone's right to die in character.

Some of the stories in *Dying with Love* are happy, more are sad, others are humorous, all are bitter-sweet.

There's ten-year-old Katy who, at her own request, was buried in her favourite red tutu and ballet shoes; the mother who told the nurse that clean teeth wouldn't matter where her Declan was going; Joan, whose grieving for her father's death was triggered by the photograph of a robin; and beautiful Julia who finally decided to forget her figure and to indulge her sweet tooth.

Dying with Love grew out of a radio documentary for RTE 1 of the same title which had evolved from my friendship with a haemophiliac suffering from the AIDS virus. His progression from disbelief and anger to an acceptance of the inevitability of his own death was the inspiration for this book.

Patricia O'Reilly
September 1992

FOREWORD

Death is part of life. Dying is part of living. Yet most of us fear death and would rather not talk about it. For most of our lives we believe and act as though death is something that happens "to other people", but not to us or ours. Then, one day, life brings death out of the closet. A fatal accident, a diagnosis of terminal illness, a cot death – and suddenly we are confronted by what we have so successfully avoided until that moment, and there is no escape.

What in death and dying do people fear? As human beings we share an existential fear of the finality of death and of the fact that it is such an absolute unknown. In addition, some fear the consequences of the eternal judgment which they believe awaits them. For most, however, the fear relates to the process of dying, how it's going to be rather than what might or might not happen afterwards. We fear the physical pain and distress, the emotional pain of separation from loved ones, the dependence and loss of control which we imagine lie ahead. What is more, for many, these fears may have been compounded by an experience of watching a loved one die badly, perhaps in pain or unsupported and alone. It is fully understandable, therefore, that we put death in a dark closet, as far as possible out of sight and out of mind.

Sadly, this is not a great solution. Feelings that are locked away do not like it. They tend to take on a life of their own, increasing in intensity as time goes by and biding their time until the day they can wreak their revenge on their captor. Put simply, if we do not look at our normal human fear of death and dying, these fears will get worse with time and will one day come back to haunt us. That time may be when we are facing our own death or the death of someone close to us, when uncontrolled fear can lead to additional unnecessary suffering and distress for all involved, as well as missed opportunities.

So what, one might well ask, do people who are dying or bereaved need to make the whole process a little easier for them?

Dr Cicely Saunders, pioneer of the modern hospice movement, tells the story of a young Polish man who was inspirational to her as she became increasingly aware of the unmet needs of the dying patients on the hospital wards where she worked and planned towards developing a system of care especially designed to meet these needs. The young man was called David Tasma and he was dying of cancer. One day, while sitting and chatting with David, Dr Saunders, desperately wanting to do all she could for him, asked him to tell her what else she could do to help. He replied, "I only want what is in your heart and in your mind". This statement became a motto of sorts for the developing hospice movement, emphasising that what people needed in their dying was more than tender, loving care, they needed *effective,* loving care.

Effectiveness has to do with competence which in turn has to do with bringing skilled care to people who are terminally ill, as well as to their families and friends at this time and afterwards, if needs be, in bereavement. It is rarely if ever true to say to one who is dying or bereaved, "I am sorry but there is nothing more I can do to help you". The competent intervention may take the form of some simple or sophisticated procedure to relieve pain, it may mean time spent talking openly with the person who is dying answering questions about what is happening or about what is likely to happen or it could take the form of a meeting between the family and the caring team. No matter where or by whom this care is offered there is so much that can be done to make the process less painful and less frightening and so transform it from a time of miserable existence to a time for living.

Cicely Saunders writes, "the real presence of another person is a place of security". To illustrate this she gives the following example: "A child separated from his mother may be quite safe, but he feels very insecure. A child in his mother's arms during an air raid may be very unsafe indeed, but he feels quite secure. We have to give all patients that feeling of security in which they can begin, when they are ready, to face unsafety". Perhaps this, then, is what David Tasma was seeking in asking for "what is in your heart"? While the dying and their families need professional competence to remove the clutter of unnecessary suffering and distress which is literally and metaphorically crowding out their "living-room", they simultaneously need the presence of another person who is prepared to stay with them in their shared humanity. This can bring real encouragement and consolation to the one who is suffering and ease the burden of isolation felt by so many at such a time. In the words of the psalmist, "deep calls to deep in the roar of waters".

While competence and caring can alleviate so much of the unnecessary distress associated with dying and bereavement, there is yet another way of making this process less feared and so less awful. That is by naming the fears, by openly discussing these topics, by providing information, and by educating patients, families and professionals.

It is in this context that *Dying With Love* is a welcome addition to the growing body of literature on death and dying. Patricia O'Reilly's sensitive use of case histories and anecdotes as she discusses the many relevant issues surrounding this topic ensures that this is a book not only rooted in reality, but in a particularly Irish reality. By discussing subject matter that is normally taboo, by separating fact from unhelpful fiction and by offering solid and practical advice this book will help to exorcise much unhelpful and unneeded fear of death and dying and so be a source of support and reassurance to many.

Dr Michael Kearney
Our Lady's Hospice
Dublin, 1992

1

The Stroke of Death

Death is an inescapable truth of life. The act of dying is the most personal and human act of our lives. Even though we may be at home and surrounded by loved family members, we are completely on our own. Nobody else can die for us. If, as so many of us believe, life is just an apprenticeship for death then the most important act of our earthly life is its last. This is when becoming yields to being and living becomes dying. When we rationalise, we know that death is the inevitable consequence of living, yet inevitability does not bring acceptance, willingness or even comprehension. Most of us are terrified of this step into the unknown and we worry about how we'll die, in what circumstances and with whom.

Too often the process of dying is perceived as a time that may be riddled with physical pain, bodily impairment and mental anguish. But this need not be so. The needs of dying patients are both physiological and emotional: the former is to do with coming to terms with body adjustments and the latter, which is greatly affected by the various stages of dying, is about being complete as a person and gaining peace of mind.

Modern medicines have worked wonders with total pain control, and when dying is accepted, it can become a time of heightened perceptions and growing spirituality. The English poet, Francis Bacon, wrote, "I know many wise men that fear to die, for the change is bitter. But I do not believe that any man fears to be dead, but only the stroke of death". As far back as the sixteenth century, then, it was recognised that the fear of dying is a specific attitude towards the process of dying and is not related to the fact of death.

It is often asked whether it's harder to die or to witness death. To some people this may seem cynical and hypocritical; nevertheless, it has its justification when the contact with the dying is an intimate one. To enter the dying person's world, it's necessary to differentiate between the actual *process* of dying and the *act* of dying.

While dying at home may theoretically be the ideal situation, sometimes this is just not possible. Bob's wife June had a particularly painful form of cancer that necessitated hospitalisation, but after her death she was brought home for the night and it was from there that her remains went to the church. That's the way Bob wanted it and today, several years later, he's glad it happened, both for his sake and for the sake of their four children.

Jamie, too, wants to die at home, because he says that if he dies in hospital, he'll be put into a body bag and he's scared stiff of that. The day he was diagnosed as being HIV positive, he lost all hope. He was afraid to live and afraid to die. He was bitter and resentful, demanding of God to know why it had happened to him. He wasn't a drug addict or a homosexual, he just had the misfortune to be born haemophiliac and the even greater misfortune to be on the receiving end of Factor 8 when he had his appendix out.

While the majority of people are more afraid of the way of their dying than of the actual act of dying, Jamie was equally terrified of both. He spent the next two years behind a closed door and says that when he was diagnosed as having full-blown AIDS it was almost a relief. He had all the associated symptoms of AIDS, such as hepatitis, pneumonia, one infection after another, inability to eat and gradual weakening of limbs. As his body weakened so did his spirit. And he says, "The fear was worst at night when I couldn't sleep. I'd wallow in negative memories, thinking I'd never make love to my wife again; hating having to leave the children, just locking into misery. The dark night of the soul – that was me".

Then an opportunity presented itself for him to go on a pilgrimage to Medjugorje. He was a reluctant pilgrim and an unlikely traveller, but he was at the "no hope" stage when anything was better than his present circumstances. "In Medjugorje, I found my God. I got acceptance and a strange brand of spirituality", he says. "The night terrors went. Suddenly I was no longer afraid and I was able to replay over and over again all the wonderful memories I have. When I'm not sleeping now I remember going to Dollymount with my father, the big bags of bulls' eyes we'd buy and my mother giving us lackery because we couldn't eat our dinner; fishing in mountain streams; dancing with my wife; and when our three children were born. For me now death is just like a caterpillar changing into a butterfly, or going from one room to another, but I want it to happen at home".

Catholic funeral rites
Catholic funeral rites have recently been updated in Rome and have been brought more in line with today's

thinking. The Church claims to be balanced in its acknowledgement of pain and the human situation. While the new rites recognise the grief of those left behind, they also aim to bring the gospel into the grieving condition.

In the new order, the remains become an icon, an image of what that person was in life. Death is seen as a journey from this life to the next. Central to this is the notion that we've already made the journey: when we were baptised we died with Christ, then rose to a new life with him, and in death we're joined to him. In the new rite, the transfer of the remains can be led by either a priest or a lay person. It includes a prayer for the closing of the coffin, with the suggestion that this is a private time, mainly for those closest to the deceased. Another theme that emerges is that death is a farewell by the community. Now, when the remains are brought to the church, they're made welcome at the door. At the foot of the altar a white pall, symbolising dignity and equality, is put on the coffin, and a paschal candle is lit. During the celebration of the funeral Mass, the congregation and the deceased are united through worship in the presence of God. At the end of the Mass is the final commendation, with the congregation perceiving that the sins of the dead person are being absolved. The farewell, with the singing of "May the angels lead you into Paradise", brings earthly and heavenly community together.

The last rites for children are designed to bring comfort to parents. They now include the option to name a stillborn child as part of the transfer of the remains; both baptised and non-baptised infants are acknowledged; with the death of an older child, the option exists to use the adult pastoral rite, if deemed more appropriate; and flexibility is built in to the last rites for the handicapped, as the more childlike service would often be more appropriate than the adult version.

Words and phrases

Philosophers and theologians down the ages have stated in their different ways that death is the road one travels towards non-being, towards physical annihilation. Death is the actual state of non-being. It's difficult for us to conceptualise our own death, our own state of nonentity, but it's relatively easy for us to conjure up the non-being of another person. We can, however, and often all too vividly, conceive of the process of dying and so, because imagination knows no bounds, we have a greater dread of the process of dying than of death itself. The statement in the novel *Amelia*, by Henry Fielding: "It hath often been said, that it is not death, but dying, which is terrible", is as true now as it was when it was first published in 1751.

Death belongs to life as does birth, but while birth is perceived as a beginning, and a celebration, death is viewed by those who don't believe in life hereafter as an end and a time of grieving. The language of birth has become part of our private and public lives, but death is cloaked in privacy, though it does receive regular media and fictional airings. Sigmund Freud claimed that "death is an abstract concept with a negative content"; Twentieth century writer Arnold Toynbee wrote, "that for man death is incongruous and humiliating". Every death is a reminder to the living of their own certain fate. Fear of social reaction can inhibit talking about death, and our own fear may prevent us from even thinking about it. But like so many hidden experiences once brought into the open, thoughts and reactions to death are universal.

The cross-section of people surveyed for this book had no difficulty believing that we would all die. Some opted for the everlasting life concept; others for total oblivion; more felt that while death was final, we remained in those we left behind. Our Western embarrassment, our view that death is a private matter, and our silence, seem peculiar to our culture and century. And yet never is the spontaneous language of death required more greatly than in the hour of our need.

There's a lot to be said for times past when death was called death, and when in Ireland the ceremony of dying and wakes were interlinked, all part of the burial ritual, allowing grieving to be thorough and noisy. Down the ages, a variety of words, secular and sacred, have been used to talk of death. In the so-called sophistication of the twentieth century many people have tried to avoid the subject completely. To cope with avoidance a new and evasive language has been developed, and the rise and rise of bereavement counselling groups reflects this lack of openness and our lack of knowledge about the dying process and death.

Many of the words and phrases used to describe death over the years are rooted in religious belief. Christianity has been the dominant persuasion in the West and for Christians, death is inextricably tied up with judgment, the soul, salvation, heaven, hell and eternal life. As an afterlife is central to Christian belief, death has always been an optimistic and victorious part of the dialogue. "So when this corruptible shall have put on incorruption, and this mortal shall have put on immortality, then shall be brought to pass the saying that is written. Death is swallowed up in victory" (1 Co 15:54).

In secular circles, euphemisms for dying and death have been used for a long time. Shakespeare used a variety of phrases and words: "Shuffled off his mortal coil"; "come to dust" ; "exits", etc. His contemporary, John Donne, opened a poem with the line, "As virtuous men pass mildly away", clearly seeing the phrase "pass mildly away" as an evocative way of describing the gentle death of virtuous men. In Dicken's *David Copperfield* Mrs Micawber tells David that her mamma "had departed this life" and that her papa had "expired".

Dying and death have been the subjects of comment from the historic sublime to the modern ridiculous. In the seventeenth century Alexander Pope, in "The Dying Christian to his Soul", wrote

> Vital spark of heav'nly flame!
> Quit, oh quit this mortal frame:
> Trembling, hoping, ling'ring, flying,
> Oh the pain, the bliss of dying.

A hundred years later, Mozart claimed that death, "is the key which unlocks the door to true happiness". In the nineteenth century Matthew Arnold decided that "truth sits on the lips of dying men". In 1910 British novelist E.M. Forster said that, "Death destroys a man, the idea of Death saves him".

While the main focus in Irish literature is on national consciousness, there are some fine examples of various

attitudes to death in the writings of W.B.Yeats, J.M.
Synge and Patrick Kavanagh. Yeats celebrates "the
silent kiss that ends short life or long", and in more
sombre mood in "Death" writes,

> A man awaits his end
> Dreading and hoping all;
> . . . He knows death to the bond –
> Man has created death.

In *The Playboy of the Western World*, Synge treats death
irreverently – Christy emerges as a hero, because he's
supposed to have killed his father; Widow Quin is
known to have murdered her husband and there's also
a reference to the hanging of a dog, just for the fun of it.
In *Memory of my Father*, Kavanagh talks about having
"fallen in love with death".

One of the tales of death which is strong in the folk-
lore of the south of Ireland is set in an unknown village
where the local priest officiated at the wedding of a
young couple. In due course a daughter was born to
them, was baptised and died. A year later they had a
son, who also died three days after baptism. The parents were very upset and sought consolation from their
priest. He had few words with which to comfort them
as he couldn't talk about death from personal experience. Then the husband was stricken with a terminal
illness and as he lay dying the priest asked him to
return and tell him what death was like. This he duly
did reporting, "The dying was worse than the death
and I'm in heaven and it's beautiful". The priest said, "I
knew you'd get to heaven. You lived a good life."
"That's not necessarily so", said the man, "I wouldn't

be here, except that my children prepared the way for me."

The priest thought long and hard, eventually resigned his parish and went to a far-off land where he married and had a son who died at a few weeks of age. The couple's second child also died within days of being baptised. One day when the wife returned, her husband was gone. She found this strange, as he'd always been a good and caring husband and she determined to find him. The only place she knew he was sure to be was at Mass, as he never missed a Sunday or a holy day. She visited all the churches in her country and then travelled the world seeking him. Eventually she came to Ireland and there she found him one Sunday morning.

He looked at her, smiled and bade her come home with him. When they reached the presbytery, he asked his housekeeper to make ready their bedroom with fresh linen and flowers. He and his wife retired. When the housekeeper went up at noon the following day, she found the door locked. Having received no response to her knock, she finally pushed the door in. The couple were lying on the bed. Resting on each of their lips was a brightly coloured butterfly.

History

In most religions the act of dying and the moment of death throughout history have been recognised as being of the utmost importance. From the fifteenth century, there has been a pan-European interest in "the art of dying well". Popular illustrations from the time are of an angel and a demon hovering on either side of the dying person. Down the ages, Christians have always put great store on preparing for a "good death". This involves the dying person's close contact with the priest for last confession, absolution and anointing with consecrated oil, known as the "anointing of the sick". In many places, it was believed that during the last moments of life the devil lurked around the death-bed ready to seize the unprepared soul as it emerged with the dying person's last breath.

There are several beliefs, specific to certain localities, which have been passed from generation to generation and many are rooted in sympathetic magic. If a candle burned in such a way as to form a hood around the flame, this was known as a "winding sheet" and was a forewarning of death. The same message was carried by coffin-shaped folds in linen or cinders thrown out of a fire, a picture falling from its hook, a door opening by itself, or unaccountable animal or bird behaviour.

Practices and beliefs surrounding death have symbolic as well as practical meanings. Almost all customs seem to have operated on more than one level. With regard to ritual eating in the corpse's presence, prevalent in several rural areas, many historians draw the comparison between it and the Eucharist. Indeed there was also a belief that every sip of wine drunk at a funeral represented a sin committed by the dead person and so drinking brought about absolution.

There's a funeral story that's often told in Galway by old people and it varies slightly in the telling. It illustrates the simultaneous existence of belief, sophistication and scepticism in relation to dying. The gist of the story is that when Chrissie was dying, she gave her best friend, Mary, a packet of letters and asked her to make sure that they were put into the coffin with her just before it was closed. Chrissie was regarded as a bit of a local character – she'd never married, though the whole townland knew that she and her family had hopes of the local doctor's son. For a while they were inseparable. Then he went away. At first the letters came regularly, then they dwindled to a few times a year and, finally, more than thirty years before Chrissie lay dying, they stopped altogether. Chrissie never spoke about it and even now she had no need to tell Mary who the letters were from. Difficult as it is to believe, but with the angst of the dying, and the waking and funeral preparations, Mary forgot. For several months she was very distressed and wracked her brain for an idea to remedy her omission. It was only when she heard that the postman from the next parish was dying that she knew she had a solution. She cycled over, explained her quandary to his wife and then to him. He said he'd be more than delighted to deliver the letters to Chrissie when he got to heaven. Indeed, he felt that having them would guarantee his own admission.

Rather contrived rituals associated with death and mourning reached a peak of refinement and detail at the end of the last century. Death was surrounded by ostentation and sentimentality (though this would have a reaction in the twentieth century's "forbidden death"), a controlled way of expressing grief. And it's now thought that perhaps it prevented a great deal of permanent suffering. In Queen Victoria's grief when her husband, Prince Albert, died, she half pretended that he was still alive. She kept every object in their private rooms as they had been when he was there, and went to the extreme of having his clothes laid out and his shaving water brought in each morning.

In earlier centuries death was a problem shared. Families were bigger and they were more closely knit. In the early part of this century our "forbidding" of death or thoughts of death was our particular culture's way of dealing with the fear of dying. Families were becoming smaller and scattered all over the country, in some cases all over the world, and the support mechanism was no longer in place. Rapid developments in medicine and increases in life expectancy have led to the belief that old age is the only natural cause of death. This has been described as producing "a death denying society". Indeed such classification can include the health care professions, where many would agree that "if there is any way to prolong the life of a patient, even for a second, it must be taken". One of the grey areas in health care is the extent to which the patient and family are taken into account. In extreme cases it can be said that modern technology enables us to keep the dead alive, and hospitals allow us to remove them from the living.

2

LIVING WHILE DYING

In Ireland only forty per cent of the population die at home. Yet research shows that most of us, if given the option, would choose to die at home, surrounded by our family and our possessions. Home is where we've chosen to live and where we feel secure. The familiar surroundings encourage living while dying.

Joan remembers her mother leaving home to go to hospital to die. "It was heartbreaking to watch her. She went into each room, touched familiar objects, and all the time the tears were rolling down her cheeks and our cheeks. She told us about making stock for soup and asked us to make sure that the birds had food during the winter. And this was only May. It would have been so much easier for her – and indeed for all of us – if she'd been able to die at home, but that wasn't really possible, as her particular form of cancer needed hospital care at that time".

Why hospital?
In many cases, including Joan's mother, hospital admission is necessary to provide adequate care, but in many more cases it is much more satisfactory and eminently feasible for the dying person to be cared for at home. When a terminally ill patient is moved from home to hospital, in addition to loss of familiarity and freedom, an element of hope is also lost. Most dying patients

know of their predicament and their move from home will be for many the final nail in their coffin.

The terminal stage of dying begins at the moment when the doctor utters the words, "There is nothing more we can do". When Phyllis was told that Rory had only about a month to live, she asked to take him home. "Mainly because I wanted him to die in our bedroom and in the bed where our children were conceived, and also because I felt the hospital staff had already started to withdraw from him". This medical withdrawal frequently happens as doctors and nurses, who are conditioned to cure, often feel that they have failed when a cure is no longer possible.

Apart from providing security, being at home allows the patient to eat when and what he wishes, to sleep when necessary and to choose his company. Many other freedoms have already been lost such as freedom to work, indulge in sport, go for a pint or even just walk the dog. A ward routine in hospital will add to this loss of freedom and increase a sense of dependence.

Public expectation of hospital as the appropriate place to die has increased over the years. The practical reasons are many and varied. Hospitals can offer continuous nursing care; some techniques of pain relief such as local radiotherapy or neuro-surgical blocks can only be carried out there and the family doctor may feel that his specialist colleagues have more to offer. Yet, recent studies suggest that unless care is exceptional, one-fifth of patients dying in hospital endure a distressing amount of physical discomfort for an appreciable proportion of the time.

However socio-economic changes and the dispersing,

disintegrating family are the factors that contribute most towards people dying in hospital. An increasing number of elderly people now live alone; where they live with their family, family members often find that they are not capable of caring for a dying relative. The majority of children no longer live within easy distance of the parental home. Many of the wives of married sons have full or part-time jobs. Unmarried children have neither time nor suitable accommodation to nurse an elderly parent.

When talking about dying at home, it is almost logical to assume that the patients are victims of cancer or AIDS, as some degree of preparation for death is possible. What is little realised is that eighty per cent of people with Motor Neuron Disease (MND) also die at home, simply because there are no hospital facilities for them. There is widespread fear of both cancer and AIDS, with a one in five risk of dying from cancer and still unknown chances of contracting AIDS. For most people the words cancer and AIDS arouse a set of closely related fears: a lingering death, intolerable pain, inevitable helplessness. This need not be so.

Dick's story

When Dick was sixty-seven he was diagnosed as having cancer of the rectum, and he was terrified of dying in hospital. His son John and daughter-in-law Mary, who lived around the corner, were equally full of fear for him. John vividly remembers his mother's death seven years earlier. "We were devastated by the experience of her dying without ever leaving hospital, just six weeks after being diagnosed. She seemed to be in constant pain and we felt completely frustrated".

During surgery, it was discovered that the tumour had spread to Dick's bladder and couldn't be completely removed. "It wasn't so much a decision as an inevitability that, despite having two toddlers, we agreed to move in with him and to take care of him in his own home", says Mary. "The nurse came every morning and we managed ourselves in the evening. Neighbours and friends were great and we'd more nursing support than we needed. Our main problem was whether Dad ought to be told. Knowing his fears, we thought it best not to say anything unless he asked."

As predicted by the consultant, several months after the operation, Dick became unable to walk without pain. John and Mary moved his bed into the front room and got him a wheelchair. "My biggest fear was getting up in the morning and finding Dad dead on the floor. I often did find him on the floor because he insisted on trying to get out of bed as soon as he woke up, despite being unable to stand", says John. "It had become an obsession with him and it caused Mary and myself a lot of worry."

One of the problems that had arisen during John's mother's terminal phase was that the whole family couldn't visit her at the one time. "Although we were made to feel welcome and visiting rules were relaxed, we realised that it did cause problems for the staff who have to cope with large numbers of often distressed people."

John and Mary had no such problem at home. Their house became the focus of the family and extended family and, indeed, friends. The children were a source of stimulation and "normalised" the situation. Their daughter was just starting to read and practised on her grandfather at every opportunity. Regularly in the evening, Dick would lie in bed in the living-room and inveigle whoever was around into playing Scrabble, which he invariably won.

Dick deteriorated slowly. Medically he was monitored constantly and his medication adjusted according to his needs. Although he was conscious and able to express his wishes, even towards the end, he never spoke about dying or mentioned cancer. During the latter stages, there was always someone with him throughout the day and, at night, John and his brother took it in turns to sleep on the sofa in the same room, give him drinks and make him comfortable.

"The weekend before he died, Dad didn't seem to be in any pain, despite being very weak and tired, but we knew he was worsening slowly", says John. On the Tuesday, while the nurse was changing his pyjama top, his breathing pattern worsened and within minutes he was dead. "It was a wonderful death for him. We felt we should be celebrating rather than grieving."

Declan's story
Declan was the apple of his parents' eyes. Kathleen and Paul were used to him coming and going as he wished. He filled the house with his friends and they'd sit around smoking and drinking innumerable cups of tea. He had a great penchant for jewellery, but he's best remembered by all who knew him for his vitality and zest for life.

As far as Kathleen can remember, Declan was never really sick and even when he went into St James' hospital, the family didn't worry too much. While he seemed weak, he was in great form whenever they visited. However, one spring day their bubble burst. They were summoned by one of the doctors, told that their twenty-four-year-old son had AIDS, and that medically nothing further could be done. Declan hadn't wanted them to be told before, as Kathleen had high blood pressure and Paul suffered from angina.

"We just wanted to take Declan home. We thought if we loved him and cared for him enough that he'd get well again", says Kathleen. Declan came home and for a while he still enjoyed life. The end when it came happened within six weeks. When he started deteriorating physically, his Dad and his brother Alan would wash and dress him slowly and carefully, as Declan preferred not to have a nurse.

Declan's bed was brought downstairs for a few weeks, but as he went downhill he preferred to be upstairs in his old room. Despite the best intentions in the world, his family could not provide total care for him and the district nurse started coming in during the mornings for the last eight days. "She used to make Declan wash his teeth, and he hated it", remembers Kathleen. "I never pushed him too much, because I knew that where he was going clean teeth wouldn't matter."

One day Declan told Alan that he wanted to die with just his immediate family around him. "We'll never forget the day he died", says Kathleen. "He'd been doing a lot of groaning and was very restless. The nurse had made him comfortable in the morning, but she called back again at lunchtime and said to Paul that it might be a good idea to get a night nurse. We knew Declan wouldn't want a nurse with him at night – he was reluctant enough during the day. I wanted to take care of him, as usual, but she insisted". The nocturnal habits of the family were that Kathleen slept under an extra duvet on the bed beside Declan, while Paul dozed in a rocking chair.

During the evening preceding his death, Declan had quietened down and Kathleen thought he was asleep. "I was downstairs when the night nurse arrived. I took one look at her in the uniform and told her that she couldn't wear that around Declan. She didn't seem to mind, she said she'd have a quick look at him and come back down for a cup of tea. A few seconds later she called me to come quickly. When I looked at my Declan, I knew he was drawing his last breaths. I took him in my arms, started into the prayer to the Sacred Heart and Our Lady that I'd been saying with him. He looked up at me and mouthed that he loved me. Then he gave three sighs and died. I saw the spirit leaving his body and going out the window".

"People keep saying that they're sorry for us. But we're the lucky ones. We had four good months with Declan at home. If he'd been in hospital we wouldn't have experienced what we did. It was the most beautiful death I've ever seen and I know our Declan went straight to heaven", says Kathleen.

* * *

When caring for the dying happens in the home, it's usually relatives and friends who lead the nursing team, with district nurses and health visitors playing supporting roles. The underlying aim of it all is the provision of what is termed a "death in character". Death in character is a death that's achieved in comfort and dignity, with the needs of the body, mind and soul all being taken into consideration.

People's individuality is reinforced by environment, possessions, life-style and the people close to them. While the majority of terminal cases appear to know that they are dying, not all talk openly about their situation – some are not able to, others have no one who will allow them to, for more the going is easier if they do not.

Moving the bed to the living-room often helps the patient to avoid feeling isolated and excluded, but this may be discouraged by the family, as containment in an upstairs room is often part of the family mechanism for coping. While the patient is out of sight it is possible to deny the reality of their dying and to continue living relatively normally. If the bed is downstairs, the pain of reality requires constant confrontation.

The fears surrounding serious illness can be divided into five categories. Existential fears are being/non-being, loss of consciousness, loss of self-image; and extinction. The religious fears are abandonment, punishment and the unknown. Biological fears include pain, deterioration, disfigurement, incontinence and loss of sexual identity. Social fears include separation, rejection, being a financial and emotional burden, being lied to, leaving others uncared for and leaving unfinished business. Medical fears are indignity, de-personalisation, de-humanisation, misinformation, ignorance and suffering.

The knowledge of imminent death provokes powerful emotions like fear, frustration, grief and anger. Suppression will not make them disappear; on the contrary, if they are not allowed to surface and to hurt, they may cause or exacerbate physical ailments or emotional disturbance, such as insomnia and recurrent nightmares. It is easier to focus on painful thoughts and to experience the pain which they arouse with someone supportive, but this isn't easy for either party, as it's hard to stay close to someone who is expressing strong negative and painful emotions.

People close to death often choose not to talk openly to their families, reasoning that this would inevitably cause distress, which seems too painful to face in addition to their own. The family often uses the same reasoning for staying quiet. This conspiracy of silence is justified as everyone's way of protecting each other from a potentially distressing subject.

Jennifer's story

Jennifer and David had a very close and caring thirty-year marriage, yet she died of cancer without either of them ever mentioning the words "cancer" or "death". When she was diagnosed at the end of July as having advanced cancer of the colon with secondaries in the liver, her life expectancy was estimated to be in the region of four months. David decided that she should not be told and a rather elaborate tale was concocted to deal with any questions she might ask. The deception wasn't necessary. She never referred to her operation, though she did talk about getting better. All her life she'd been very active, always busy doing things around the house and in the garden. Her pattern was early rising, getting all her "bits and pieces", as she called them, done in the morning and since David had retired they went out somewhere each afternoon.

35

She came home from hospital in the middle of August. It was a glorious late summer and early autumn. She rose mid-morning – David reckoned each day it was more and more difficult for her to get up – and they went for little walks or drives in the afternoon. She'd always dressed smartly and put a lot of attention into her grooming. She organised a hairdresser to visit her at home; kept her nails varnished and when she grew noticeably thinner, she bought some new clothes. Gradually she became weaker and though she'd always enjoyed good food, she no longer seemed interested. But she expressed pleasure at the dainty trays she received and insisted on eating on her own. It was a few weeks before David realised that she was flushing most of the food down the toilet.

"Gradually she stopped walking when we were out in the afternoons and would just sit in the car looking out to the sea", says David. "The last time we went for a drive, she seemed to have difficulty sitting up and when I suggested going home she agreed immediately, but asked if we could go by the coast road. She'd always loved the sea." She talked a lot about a spring holiday in the sun and was making plans for a trip to Lourdes later on. "Some of the family felt she should be told she had terminal cancer, but I wouldn't permit this under any circumstances, and indeed had to warn some visitors to be careful on the subject", says David. "My horror was that a stage would be reached, if she developed extreme pain, that she could no longer be nursed at home, but thankfully this didn't happen."

Jennifer gradually drifted downhill, the nurse started coming in daily and David remembers that time as "Jennifer sleeping a lot". Her medication was constantly adjusted to take her increasing pain into account. She slipped into a coma and died in her sleep surrounded by her family at the beginning of November. "Looking back now I wonder did she know she was dying, but for our sakes kept her feelings 'bottled up'", says David. But he has never doubted his decision not to tell her that she had terminal cancer. "I think of her daily and of the wonderful life we had together."

Sometimes, as in Jennifer and David's case, the element of mutual pretence is the best way of coping with impending death. Others may realise that holding back in this way does not make it easier to cope and often regret the lack of sharing. Some couples who have had an honest, open relationship may grow to hate the thought of their final parting being marred by deceit. Others feel they simply cannot cope with their overwhelming fear of death or bereavement without their partner's support.

Denial

Denial can be a valuable defence mechanism which the dying frequently employ, particularly during the earlier stages of their illness. When it is used most forcibly, patients may trek from one doctor to another in an attempt to procure a different medical opinion, while others will fail to attend appointments. They may avoid any discussion about their diagnosis or prognosis, desperately trying to live a totally normal life. Even thinking about their death may be avoided, and hyperactivity is common, every waking moment being filled with activity so that there is no time for painful thoughts to surface.

Charlotte's story

The operation to remove the malignant tumour from Charlotte's oesophagus was successful and she had four good months. But with the discovery of secondaries, the prognosis was not favourable. After many weeks of denial and non-acceptance, one evening she and her husband Robert spoke about her death. After that one occasion, they held the knowledge close, but they never spoke about it again and didn't discuss her death with her family, or his. She busied herself at a frenetic rate for as long as she could, adapting their home to make it easier for Robert to run when she was dead. She bought a microwave and a mini-freezer which she filled with one-portion casseroles and shepherd's pies; re-designed the bathroom; streamlined the kitchen; replaced shabby towels and sewed on all the shirt-buttons that she had been promising to do for years. In the meantime Robert bought a grave, swearing the staff to secrecy and insisting that no papers should be posted to their home. When the time came near for her dying, she lay in bed in her beautifully decorated room and saw her friends and extended family for the last time. The room became suffocated with flowers. The sadness between them all was unspoken until the last twenty-four hours when she told her sister that she didn't want to die. Her going in the end was peaceful enough, though for a few hours she was into the "grounding" syndrome of needing to feel the floor under her feet.

It was much later that the family discovered that Charlotte had been to her church, and had asked the parish priest to use the main, rather than the customary side gate, for her funeral. She'd also left an envelope with the undertaker, specifying the readings she'd like and her choice of music.

* * *

However openly someone may have discussed the future on other occasions, periods of denial may still occur, perhaps as the only means of defence, when the full impact of reality seems intolerable. This is only reckoned to be harmful when employed continuously, causing the painful feelings about dying to be suppressed. Intermittent denial calls for sensitivity that permits it one moment and the next supports the patient in dealing with his awareness of truth.

For months, Peter, the father of two young children in his early forties, had refused to accept his fairly imminent death. Suddenly one evening while he and his wife, Doreen, were watching television, he started talking. He told her how guilty he felt about leaving her to cope alone; his grief about not being there to see his family grow up and to support them; fear about the course his illness would take and the manner of his death; and anger about having his life curtailed so prematurely.

Doreen found that her husband's fears were her fears. They talked long into the night, cried together and comforted each other. Doreen felt that Peter had reached peaceful acceptance of the inevitable. Next morning when she brought him his breakfast tray, he said: "When I'm completely better and all this is behind us, we'll put a conservatory on to the gable wall and take the children to Crete on holidays." The big burst of reality had been too painful for him to face all at once.

The reality

The terminally ill are often emaciated, frequently bedridden for long periods due to weakness, pain or paralysis and are likely to experience a wide variety of symptoms, ranging from constipation to the pain of nerve compression. Comfort is not something which is easily achieved and skilled physical nursing care is of paramount importance. This includes bathing, protecting pressure areas, the care of the mouth, bowel management, positioning in bed, movement and exercise and attention to diet and fluid intake – much the same as the care of anyone who is seriously ill.

Nothing beats human contact – someone sitting by the bedside, the reassurance of a hand being held and quiet conversation all have a very calming effect. It's a time when many fears can come out of hiding and when the unspoken can finally be spoken. The relationships which develop between dying patients and family members can be deep and valuable, never achieved before and unlikely ever to have happened without the given set of circumstances.

Many people become confused for a short period before the end of their lives and they're often greatly relieved by an explanation. Even confirmation of a brain tumour can be less frightening than the fear of going mad. It's important not to cause humiliation by exposing loss of memory and disorientation. Information about where and who the patient is and what time of day it is, should be given frequently in the course of conversation.

Collusion with confused thinking is reckoned to be best avoided, as it's important to keep as much in touch with reality as possible. An established daily routine, with regular mealtimes, bath times, visitors and bed-time will increase the feelings of security. Since making choices may be difficult, some decisions will have to be made on the dying person's behalf, but this should be done with maximum tact and respect. People who are confused are as easily hurt as anyone else.

Relatives can experience guilt about their lack of patience or their supposed inadequacy in caring for the patient, about their failure to notice early symptoms, which they feel could have led to a better prognosis, or guilt about hurtful, selfish behaviour which may have occurred throughout the relationship. This distress may be heightened by the exhaustion of weeks without ade-quate sleep. Also the relative's feelings about his own mortality and death will be aroused by the patient, and in the long term it's better to acknowledge and express these feelings.

Over-pampering and smothering the patient is nearly as bad as neglect. Few people enjoy being treated and regarded as invalids, especially when their days are numbered. Quality of life, not quantity, is what counts now. To achieve the maximum quality of life, rehabili-tation should be the aim of treatment until the last lap.

A week after Jack returned from hospital after being told that there was nothing more that could be done for him medically, he stuck his head around the sitting room door and announced to his daughter that he was off to the pub for a drink. She reacted with horror, but her father told her that he intended to live until he died. This he did, enjoying a regular flutter at the grey-hounds, and living his last days in the manner to which he was accustomed.

Josie hung onto her role as homemaker until the last

weeks of her life by planning the meals, writing out shopping lists, organising a family rota for cleaning, washing and ironing. Even though she couldn't carry out any of the physical work herself, she had a sense of usefulness and belonging as she prepared vegetables, paid bills or did the mending from her armchair or even sitting up in bed.

Not surprisingly, relatives are sometimes overwhelmed by the sheer enormity of the task of caring for a severely debilitated, bedridden person. As the days and weeks progress, they can feel isolated and very alone. As every, even amateur, psychologist knows, distress can form a complete block to comprehension and very little information is understood or retained if the associated fears are not dealt with first. Even if the loved one is not accepting the inevitability of death, it is necessary for the carers to be able to communicate their feelings freely with either the social worker, nurse or doctor.

3

LOVE MADE VISIBLE

Since the mid 1960s hospice or palliative medicine has emerged as an essential, rather than a peripheral, aspect of Irish health care. The primary focus has been on patients with advanced cancer, one of the most common causes of death in Ireland. Hospice or palliative care is a concept or philosophy of care which can be applied in different ways and which includes certain essential ingredients. These are effective symptom control, good communication, care of the family before and after bereavement, spiritual care and a multi-disciplinary team approach.

The success of the hospice movement can be described as a reaction to too much inappropriate treatment, which is seen by many as exacerbating the problems of chronic pain, unpleasant symptoms, dependency, fear and loss of self-esteem. At some stage in every terminal case, active treatment becomes irrelevant to the needs of the dying person. If the only foreseeable course of the illness is towards the patient's death, then this terminal stage requires appropriate care, which is directed not towards cure, but towards the care of the dying patient.

Home Care Service
The Home Care Service in Harold's Cross was set up in January 1985 as a natural progression from the developing Palliative Care Service. A Home Care team can adequately serve many terminally-ill patients so that

they can die in the familiar surroundings of their own homes. Patients must be referred either by their doctor or by a hospital and are seen by the Home Care team within ten days of referral. Another requirement is that there must be at least one adult at home capable of caring for the terminally ill person. At any one time Hospice Home Care cares for in the region of thirty-five to forty patients.

As normal a lifestyle as possible is very much the aim of the Hospice Home Care team. The success of Home Care lies in the physical and psychological assessment of each patient and the management of symptoms. Despite popular belief, pain isn't always present with cancer. But where it is, medication can keep the patient above the pain threshold.

As a diabetic needs insulin, likewise a person with pain needs the appropriate medication to live life fully. This is part of the palliative philosophy. There must also be an appreciation of the fear of pain when undertaking the management of it. The aim of Home Care is to work towards alleviating symptoms within the shortest space of time possible. The family unit, not the patient in isolation, is dealt with, as it is well recognised that the more support and encouragement families have the more confidence they gain in their role as carers.

Home Care operates within a ten-mile radius of Our Lady's Hospice. The service which is non-denominational, operates twenty-four hours a day, seven days a week. Demand for the service far exceeds what the small team can accomplish. But if the team grew too big, its members would be unable to offer vital support to each other.

Fear, loneliness and feelings of isolation are usual with cancer. Once the physical and emotional symptoms have been managed, the patient is encouraged to take charge of his own life and to set realistic goals. Sometimes, as the Home Care team have discovered, it isn't easy to get the family to draw back. They've been so used to having to do everything for the patient that they just can't believe he's feeling so much better and is able do things for himself.

Ronald's story

Despite being paralysed from the chest down, Ronald is positively concerned with living. Dividing his time between his bed and his wheelchair, he has no self-pity and his manner is forthright and positive. He's the kind of man for whom there's no incongruity in sitting up in bed wearing a collar and tie. He took retirement from his demanding executive position in the mid-1980s on health grounds and discovered the joys of gardening.

Gradually, a niggling ache in his back became a violent pain. The operation to remove a cancerous tumour in his upper spinal column left him paralysed. He required radiation treatment for post-operative sores, followed by rehabilitation in hospital. When he was discharged to his home, he was given a bed, a hoist, a wheelchair, various medications and no hope.

His wife, Betty, knew Ronald wanted to be at home, and she and their two daughters wanted him there too. But they worried about their ability to care for him. He needed regular turning in bed and, despite the medication, was breathless, nauseous and constantly coughing. With hindsight Ronald now realises that his physical symptoms were affecting his mental well-being and he became increasingly aware of his mortality and very fearful.

The family had heard about Home Care and spoke to their GP about the possibility of availing of the service. A few days later the Hospice Home Care team visited. After consultation with his GP, Ronald's symptoms were controlled, his worries alleviated and a *Pegasus* mattress dispensed with the need for constant turning. "It's great knowing there's help just a phone call away twenty-four hours a day, 365 days of the year", says Betty.

There's a great atmosphere in the house. Activity centres around Ronald, who is enthroned in the dining-room from where he can keep an eye on the running of the house. "I wouldn't have any hesitation in saying that it's being at home that makes my life worth living".

His day starts at 6.30 a.m. when his daughter makes him a cup of tea before going to work herself. At around 9 am, when Betty gets up, he has a bowl of porridge. About an hour later one of the public health nurses bathes, dresses and helps him into the wheelchair. The day passes quickly for Ronald: "I've no time to moan or to become introverted". He stays abreast of current affairs, is catching up on his reading and entertains a steady stream of visitors. Now that he can no longer garden, he has become an expert on pot plants. Out in the conservatory, he has everything to hand and spends hours pruning, potting, fertilising and slipping. He's beginning to get a bit of a name for himself in the neighbourhood as an expert and is only too delighted to pass on his knowledge.

Ronald and Betty are very well aware that if Home

Care didn't exist, he would, at best, be confined to a rehabilitation hospital. In Ronald's view, Home Care has achieved the almost impossible. He is comfortable, happy, well-adjusted and feels useful. His symptoms are constantly monitored and he and the family know that he does not have to suffer pain. As a family they're turning what could have been a disaster into an enriching experience.

Will's story

Will came to Our Lady's Hospice in Harold's Cross via the Samaritans and St Luke's cancer hospital. He was in his early forties, had lung cancer and claimed to have no family or friends. His only possession was a small Gladstone bag, from which he refused to be parted. He settled into the ward, but communicated with no one. When the staff spoke to him, he listened courteously, but never commented. His Gladstone bag never left his side.

When he thought he was unobserved, he'd lift the bag onto the bed beside him and caress it; then he began opening it and feeling the contents. One day he opened it wide, looked in and closed it with a smile. The next day he revealed its contents, a set of carpenter's tools, and began telling his story.

He'd run away to England from his home in Sligo when he was sixteen and hadn't contacted his parents since. He wasn't sure why he'd left home, but he did know that he hated school. In England he found work on a building site. The boss was an Irishman and recognised Will's skill with his hands. He paid for him to attend carpentry classes at night and eventually Will got his diploma.

As the years went by his skills increased, but he began drinking and gambling. After a while his work suffered and his employer had to let him go. He went to London where he slept rough. When he learned that he had terminal lung cancer he decided to return to Ireland. He slept rough for a while around Dublin, but eventually found the Samaritans, who got him into St Luke's and, finally, he arrived at the Hospice.

He thrived in the Hospice environment, which recognises the importance of the individual pursuing his own quality of life. He began whittling wood while still in bed and a small shed in the grounds was made available to him. With his permission the staff at the Hospice notified his mother, brothers and sisters of his whereabouts and the family had a moving reconciliation.

He began to sell his stools and lamps and used the money to go across the road to the pub to have a drink and to place a bet on the horse of his choice. One night, six months after he first came to the Hospice, he haemorrhaged. But he was in no pain and he slept peacefully for several hours afterwards. Early the next afternoon he got up, dressed and wandered down the avenue. He crossed the road, had his customary drink and placed his bet. But instead of watching the race in the pub, as was his custom, he returned to the Hospice, turned on his television and lay on his bed to see the race. His horse gambolled home at 6-1. He then closed his eyes and died.

Will's story shows the Hospice in operation. The environment allowed him to pursue his individual lifestyle unhindered. His quality of life was dependent on carpentry, having a drink and placing a bet. The staff at the Hospice recognised this and encouraged him and gave him space to be Will even in his dying.

Hospice history

The word "hospice", derived from Latin, means "a house of entertainment for strangers . . . a home of refuge". And so it was in medieval times when hospices existed to provide travellers with food and refuge to fuel them physically and spiritually for their journey. The word was revived at the turn of the century in Ireland by the Irish Sisters of Charity when they began caring for terminally-ill patients at Our Lady's Hospice in Dublin, the first of its kind in western Europe.

Love of the poor and suffering was the impelling principle of Mary Aikenhead's life, founder of the Sisters of Charity in 1815, and the inspiration for the Hospice. Aikenhead saw the poor as God's nobility and reckoned that they deserved the very best of medical treatment. She and her sisters were the first religious order to work on the streets of Dublin alleviating the suffering and sickness of the poor. Her dream of a hospital to serve Dublin's poor and sick became a reality in 1834 with the opening of St Vincent's Hospital. It was the first Catholic voluntary hospital in Ireland and ran counter to the feeling of the time.

The story goes that one of the novices who was working in Vincent's came down with cholera. She brought the disease back to the novitiate in Harold's Cross and soon another fifteen sisters were affected. Unlike so many Dubliners who caught the disease, the sisters all survived because of the excellence of the nursing. But it was decided to move to the country to guarantee the long-term health of the order. So when they went to Milltown, Harold's Cross was left vacant. The seeds of the hospice as it exists today were sown.

In December 1879 Our Lady's formally welcomed its first patients, thirty-five in number. So overwhelming were the applications for admission that six years later the foundation stone of the present Hospice was laid and the building was completed two-and-a-half years later.

Dame Cicely Saunders is internationally recognised as the pioneer of the modern hospice movement. She began her work in pain control in advanced cancer with the Irish Sisters of Charity in St Joseph's Hospice in East London during the 1950s. She has been responsible for research, teaching and a new approach to caring, particularly for families. St Christopher's Hospice in London, which has provided the pattern for so many hospice units, evolved in response to the request of a dying patient. David Tasma, a refugee from Poland who died in 1948 in a surgical ward, left the first £500 towards the hospice. He said to Dame Cicely, "I want what is in your mind and in your heart . . . I want to be a window in your home". And so he was and is.

The term "hospice movement" describes the huge increase in hospice-type service over the past twenty-five years. As today's medicine becomes more high-tech, the criticism is often levelled that in its pursuit for cure medicine has forgotten its caring origins, ignores the human dimension and is losing its very soul – all of which comes into sharp focus in the context of terminal illness. This has been recognised not just by the ordinary lay person, but also by many within the profession who identify in the hospice movement some of the qualities which brought them into medicine in the first place.

The root of the Hospice is all about re-connecting with the primary purpose of medicine which is curing illness and healing the person. In terminal cases there can be no cure, but the healing is important. Much has been said and written internationally about the spirit of the Hospice and much more will be said and written with the current growing interest in the Hospice movement. Yet it is difficult to capture a spirit in words. Perhaps the nearest is Kahlil Gibran's "Work is love made visible". From their very inception, hospices have operated in a spirit that takes account neither of race, nor creed, nor class but looks simply to the human need for help and for peace in the last days of life.

Today in Harold's Cross they hold on to the same spirit, which is born out of love, compassion, care and respect for the dignity and worth of each human person. The objective is to comfort and to console the patients and the families of the patients who seek Hospice help. The enhancement of the closing stage of life for Hospice patients is the key to the Hospice philosophy.

In Ireland, particularly Dublin, for too many people the word "hospice" has a deep-rooted stigma and, indeed, fear attached to it. This attitude is shrouded in the mists of history and ignorance and is tied in with connotations of destitution and hopelessness. Nothing could be further from the reality of the Hospice.

The Hospice today
The atmosphere in the Hospice in Harold's Cross is one of hope and caring and kindness and competence. The

walls are painted bright, cheerful colours and there are lots of modern prints and flowers and pot plants. At any one time there are about forty-six terminal cancer patients and about 110 chronically-ill elderly people, suffering from a variety of ailments.

The cancer patients are divided between St Anne's and St Charles' wards, which are complete units. The staff/patient ratio is 1:1. There are a few single rooms, but the majority of patients are in four-bed wards. There is plenty of space between each bed and for most of the patients the Hospice is home from home. Some have imported their own bedspreads and bedlinen; more have brought their own pillows; others have festooned wall space with their paintings; there are plenty of knick-knacks, photographs and mementoes.

Patients who are active are very obviously at one with the nursing staff and even those who are very sick are in no pain and have an aura of tranquillity and serenity. Every extra day is precious. Time is well-used in the Hospice. For those with an artistic bent, there are painting classes; reminiscing sessions for aspiring historians; aromatherapy for those in need of gentle relaxation; for light entertainment, there's bingo and afficionados of the body beautiful are catered for with massage, facials, pedicures and manicures.

When the weather is fine, the patients who are well enough are taken out for wheelchair walks; to listen to their chatter when they return it's as though they'd been to the most exciting place in the world. And for them they have. In the spring they've seen the clearing skies and felt the thrust of new life; in the summer they've watched the buds turn into flowers and been grateful for the warmth of the sun on their bodies; come autumn there's the magnificence of nature's colours and the vibrant nip in the air; and winter brings its own austere beauty, the trees skeletoning against the sky, the chill of snow and frost and the promise of spring.

Growing concern at the Hospice for the acute terminally ill made it advisable to separate them from the chronically sick. Palliative care came into being in 1979. It is a holistic approach to nursing, and a major breakthrough in that it allows symptoms and pain to be controlled, while at the same time providing psychological support. Comfort care, or symptom control, is an important and integral part of care of the dying. The palliative care approach offers a person who is in an unsafe situation a feeling of security. Security permits the acceptance of a feeling of lack of safety. It accomplishes what deception and denial cannot.

An important part of the Hospice's recent renaissance period has been the recognition, in 1987, by the UK-based Royal College of Physicians of palliative medicine as a sub-specialisation of general internal medicine. This move gave terminal care the status of a valued and respected part of general medical care.

Patients with advanced cancer experience a variety of symptoms, though none is a constant feature. These include, in order of relevance, pain, anorexia, constipation, dry mouth, nausea, insomnia, dyspnoea (difficulty breathing), vomiting, oedema (swelling), coughing. When somebody is in a lot of pain, they are completely taken over by it. The Hospice terms this "total pain", because it is a total experience, comprising physical, emotional, social and spiritual pain, which varies in relevance from individual to individual. By controlling that pain, the Hospice clears a space for living.

George's story

George was fifty-six when he was admitted to Our Lady's Hospice for pain control. He had a tumour on his left lung and the pain in his left shoulder extended down his arm. On admission, although he was in considerable distress, he seemed to the Hospice staff to be on reasonable and suitable doses of medication and he had also had a nerve block in the referring hospital some days previously. The appropriate physical measures had been taken, but without success.

Over the following days George spoke of his anxieties. His wife was at home caring for their granddaughter, as their daughter, whose marriage had broken up, was in hospital with a back problem. That he had not made a will was an additional worry too, as was the fact that the car tax and insurance were due, the central heating oil had to be ordered and he wanted to get cracking on the garden. Finally, one day he asked if he had cancer, adding that he had seen his brother die of cancer in so much pain that he remembered him "banging his head on the bedroom wall" in an attempt to find some relief. The Hospice staff assured him that he would never have to be in pain. George gradually began to articulate his struggle to make sense of what was happening with questions like "What did I do to deserve this?"; "Why me?"

Having been in the Hospice for less than a week, George's pain was no longer the problem that it had been, he was more comfortable and was beginning to enjoy life again. This was not the result of any specific intervention and his medication remained essentially unchanged. Rather this change came through recognition of the many different aspects of his pain and by providing the space, help and support which he and his family needed in this total pain situation. The staff at the Hospice know well that total pain like George's demands a total response. In practice this entails a willingness to work alongside professionals of other relevant disciplines in a team fashion and to use, not only the Hospice staff's medical skills, but also their very humanity as a therapeutic resource.

The palliative unit of Our Lady's Hospice focuses on skilled and loving care of the patient, coupled with sympathetic and kindly consideration for the family. It cares for about four hundred people annually, usually twice the number of women as men. The highest percentage, thirty-three men and twenty-nine women in 1989, were suffering from cancer of the bronchus and lung. The next greatest number were women with breast cancer, forty-eight, and there were a further twenty women with gynaecologically originated cancer.

Julia's story
Julia is a beautifully groomed, glamorous forty-something with bone cancer. A year ago, she was given a month to live. Over the past twelve months she has used the Hospice for symptom and pain control and in between times she is able to pick up the threads of her life at home. Her introduction to cancer was the discovery of a lump in her breast in 1985. "The consultant I was referred to by my GP dismissed me as a hysterical housewife. A year later it was discovered that I had breast cancer and liver secondaries. I spent three months in St James' Hospital".

When Julia was discharged life was more precious than ever before and she became determined to accomplish all her heart's desires. She gave up her job, enrolled in the UCD arts faculty with the ultimate aim of doing Law, and paid a visit to the Hospice. "I decided I'd like to be treated and to die there. I drove up, met Sr Francis Rose and had a chat with her. She said that I was too healthy now, but to come back when it was necessary."

Julia didn't need the Hospice for several years. After her arts degree, she gave up the idea of law and opted instead to travel around Mexico. A fall, which damaged her ribs, caused her bone cancer to be diagnosed, but she says that there was no trace of cancer in her liver at that time.

The only part of her grooming that she has become relaxed about is her weight. She reckons that at this stage there is not much harm in indulging her sweet tooth. "My family have been wonderful, but some people are too embarrassed to talk to me because I have cancer. There's a terrible stigma attached to it". She says she has a good life, though she has to spend a lot of time resting. She enjoys lunching with her friends, outings with her husband and travelling. She is living each day as it comes and is grateful for the chance to do so.

* * *

The Hospice philosophy of "living to the end" is spreading throughout Ireland with the establishment of other hospices and home care services in different parts of the country. Currently there are several free-standing hospices in the thirty-two counties, and more are planned; there is an increasing number of Home Care teams, a growing number of specified hospital beds and there are many other projects under way. At the moment palliative care, which is rapidly developing in Ireland, deals exclusively with cancer patients, though it is hoped that in the not too distant future it will provide care for the ever-increasing numbers of AIDS patients. Projects are also under way to provide palliative care to children with terminal and chronic illness, and to adults with non-malignant conditions and terminal neurological conditions.

4

THE SHARPEST CHALLENGE

Bereavement is the deepest initiation into the mystery of human life, an initiation more searching and profound than love. Love remembered and consecrated by grief is stronger than death and belongs in the eternal world. Bereavement is the sharpest challenge to our trust in God. When faith overcomes this, and given time it does, it proves once again that there is no mountain which faith cannot move. Ultimately, bereavement brings the eternal world nearer to us and makes it seem more real. This seems to be especially the case when death takes place in the home.

Alf's story
When Alf retired from the Civil Service, he pursued his hobby of gardening with the single-minded passion and meticulous detail that he had brought to his job. His care and attention paid dividends and his blooms drew admiration from far and wide. But his proudest achievement was his relationship with Rob. Rob was a robin, and after many months of gentle cajoling, he allowed Alf to hand-feed him. Alf's daughter, Joan, who lived with him, used to ring him most days from the office around lunchtime and was invariably treated to the antics of Rob that morning, and during dinner she'd get an account of his afternoon goings-on.

When Alf died suddenly and peacefully in his sleep, Joan handled the funeral arrangements efficiently, took up the threads of her own life again and hardly gave a thought to Rob, who was no longer in evidence. Several months later she went to a photographic exhibition. The photograph that caught her eye and held her attention was a picture of a robin standing on the handle of a spade. Suddenly she found her eyes filling with tears and she was overwhelmed with grief. She went to the Ladies, locked herself in, sat on a loo and cried. She mourned her loss, of her father and of the bird. She bought the photograph and it holds pride of place in her living-room today.

The dictionary defines bereavement as "to rob"; "to dispossess, particularly of immaterial things", and "to leave desolate". While Joan was left in spiritual desolation, she often talks about her father's dying as "being good" and is grateful that his death happened at home. "It was a more natural and fitting end to his life".

The consumer movement for "natural childbirth" and "natural death" regards home as the appropriate place for these events. The main argument against home births is the possible risk to the baby. This has no counterpart in home deaths.

Nancy's story

Nancy lived with her daughter May and son-in-law Robert for the last ten years of her life. She was an autocratic lady who always made her presence felt and an outsider looking in could be forgiven for thinking that May had a hard time with her. Mother and daughter were in agreement that their relationship was volatile. They recognised that their saving grace was Nancy's fondness for travel, which meant that they didn't spend too many months together under the same roof.

When Nancy had a stroke while visiting her brother

in Italy, May flew out and brought her back. Against her GP's advice she decided to keep her mother at home. In the beginning it wasn't too bad – once Nancy had made an initial recovery, she made an effort to get up and dressed, but after a few months that stopped, and she just stayed in bed. A nurse came in daily to attend to her needs. She became increasingly querulous and demanding and wanted constant company.

The Nancy/May relationship in intimacy is a classic situation in pre-bereavement. The type of intimacy – and it's immaterial whether the quality is good or bad – that develops between two people when one is incapacitated by illness and the other is attempting to meet their physical needs is rarely achieved in any other relationship. May's emotional withdrawal, though understandable, caused sadness to Nancy, who felt that she was being deserted at the very time when she most needed companionship and understanding. To further complicate communication, she was in denial that her death was fairly imminent. While May was willing to provide all Nancy's material necessities, subconsciously she fought against becoming too emotionally involved for fear that she'd be sucked into Nancy's death. She didn't know how to behave or what to say. She was also battling with an increasing sense of grief at her mother's impending death, which she felt unable to share with her mother.

The family GP persuaded her that she needed a break and assured her that her mother would be well looked after in the nursing home he recommended. Nancy begged to stay at home. With the aid of the family, an old friend and the nurse, this was possible. May and Robert were just beginning to relax on their holiday when they were sent for. Nancy wasn't expected to live for more than forty-eight hours. May was holding her hand when she died peacefully three days later. "It was amazing, the minute she died her presence was no more", says May. "I felt lonely, isolated, rootless and sad. I'd found it very difficult to cope during the last months and often wished she'd die, but when it happened I'd have given anything to have her back."

During a prolonged illness like Nancy's and, indeed, for people with Alzheimer's disease and senile dementia, some of the grieving which usually occurs during bereavement takes place while the patient is still alive. Apart from grief at the anticipated loss, there will be anxiety about the future. Not every close relationship is a good and loving one and when there has been bitterness and pain, the combination of grief at the imminent death and guilt about the sense of relief it brings can be a terrible burden to carry. May carried around a lot of unnecessary guilt in the weeks after her mother's death, mainly because she felt she should have spent more time at her mother's bedside.

* * *

Mourning is a grieving process. Mourning is more a remembering and an undoing than a forgetting. Every minute tie of memory has to be undone and something permanent and valuable recovered and absorbed from the knot. While the end is gain, the process, like all other human births, is painful and long and can be dangerous. It's also insidious in that memories can be triggered by seeming inconsequentials. Every time Jack hears an ambulance siren, he's brought back twenty years to the mad rush to hospital with his sister, who had suffered a heart attack and later died.

Jane's mother had a passion for ice-cream wafers and she particularly liked them with a cup of tea or coffee. The first time Jane did the supermarket shopping after her mother had died, when she saw the wafers stacked up beside the freezer, she was so overwhelmed with grief that she just left her loaded trolley and drove home blindly. A school friend from way back was staying with her so Jane was able to pour out thirty years' pent-up emotions and feelings about her mother, herself and her life. Afterwards she remembers feeling sad, yet refreshed and invigorated. Today she realises that joy and pleasure are easy to communicate and to accept but that grief can be shared only when it is recognised and when someone, like her old school friend, was prepared to accept the pain of her sharing.

Grief

All grief, from the most trivial to the most severe, is disabling. Both components of grief, emotional response and interruption of customary and expected activity, vary in magnitude and duration. Even the loss of a piece of jewellery causes an emotional response and an interruption in the flow of activity. The feelings may be much stronger if the jewellery was valuable and had a sentimental attachment. The grief that is suffered at the break-up of a relationship, the death of a pet or when moving house can be disabling in the short-term while it is being worked through, but if the natural grieving process is stunted the long-term effects can be disastrous.

Grieving is a natural process through which many people progress using their own resources, usually with the help and support of family and friends. Close relatives often exhibit some or all of the emotional stages through which the dying person is passing. The sense of loss begins before the actual death and anticipatory grief will be experienced as part of bereavement.

Essentially, bereavement is an experience of change and adjustment. While it involves considerable suffering, there is the potential for continued maturation of the individuals concerned. A major bereavement is an all-consuming experience and one which can be very frightening. People who are going through it often believe that they will be overwhelmed by the impact of it.

Sadly, uninhibited mourning no longer has any place in today's brave new world. In Ireland, until recently, the wake, defined as a watch or vigil beside a corpse, sometimes with revelry, was an integral part of death. Death was traditionally a community exercise, centred around the body which was laid out in the parlour or in the bedroom. After death, the body had to be washed and plugged – and the carrying out of this service was considered an honour – the shroud chosen, the best bedlinen aired, pennies laid on the eyes to keep them closed, rosary beads entwined around the fingers. Then the candlesticks had to be polished and fresh white candles lit, flowers had to be arranged, lace cloths laundered, starched and ironed. There were hams to be cooked, stout and whiskey to be provided, bread and fruit cakes to be baked, trifles to be made.

Many of these loving chores were carried out in conjunction with the family by friends and neighbours from far and wide who would come to grieve with the family. This input had another very important role. Because these "strangers" would take over the running of the house and farm or shop, it freed the family to get on with the important business of now, which was mourning. Loud lamentation was encouraged and the tradition of the keening women is well known.

During the days and nights of waking before and after the body was laid to its final rest, family members were encouraged to remember the good and the bad about the deceased. His or her oldest friends were expected to recount their memories. A comment like, "Johnny must still have his confirmation money"; or "Mary knew everyone's business" triggered story after story, some showing the deceased in a good light, others not so favourably. But the net result for the family members listening in and, indeed, contributing themselves, was that they got their loved one into healthy perspective. In times like this, the listening and talking were far from being passive activities. The quality of both demanded every last drop of concentration and empathy.

Children
Children frequently think of death as having a physical form, be it a monster, a black or white shape or a skeleton. Up to the age of three children's rationalisation of death is that the dead person went away and will never come back and they need a great deal of reassurance. From the ages of three to seven, children have a mixed

notion of death, one that is half fact and half fiction. At around the age of eleven they arrive at an acceptance of mortality and with this, the experts maintain, comes the end of innocence.

Children's instincts and intelligence are very finely tuned. They are expert at picking up vibrations in the home and reading body language accurately. Mixed signals cause them fear and distress. It's very easy for children to inherit a dis-ease about death, which they can carry with them right through life. Secrecy in a home about anything bodes no good. This is especially so regarding death. If the family pet dog dies, rather than saying, "It ran away", it's far better to explain factually what has happened, without gruesome frills. From an early age, children respond well to rituals. They love the idea of a mock funeral, with all its pomp and ceremony, and they can learn a lot from it. A shoebox can be a coffin, and the older children can be familiarised with the funeral ceremony, etc. With all children, honesty without compromise is the foundation of an adjusted adulthood.

Tom ended up in a psychiatric hospital when he was twenty-one. His parents, private, undemonstrative people, had always considered the family to be well-adjusted and they felt deeply what they considered to be a stigma. Psychotherapy disclosed that Tom had never been given the opportunity to mourn the death of his twin sister, which occurred when they were seven years old. With the best intentions in the world his parents had sent him to relatives in the country.

Describing anything to do with death to children requires clear and precise language. Euphemisms and evasions cause nothing but confusion. Children who are told that the dead person has gone away, rightly expect that person to return eventually. When people die they aren't lost and children regularly become confused at adults' ability to lose people. Phrases like "last sleep" and "sleep forever" are equally confusing and can also make the child nervous about going to sleep. Phrases like "Gone to heaven" or "gone to God" have the same connotations today as they did in the nineteenth century for French novelist Alexander Dumas. When he asked where God was and was told that he was "up in the sky", he got a gun and climbed out on to the roof with the ultimate aim of reaching the sky to shoot this God who had taken his father.

When a loved one is dying in the home, children should, ideally, have access to that person. It's vital to keep them clued into what's happening – when a vacuum is left in a child's mind it causes distress. A child should be able to put together pieces of information rather like a jigsaw. They should be told about the death of the family member – be it parent, brother, sister or grandparent – by somebody they know, love and trust. This person's attitude must be warm and loving and they must speak reassuringly and factually about death, using plain language rather than euphemisms; being careful that the children will not associate sleep or sickness with death. They should also show their own emotions naturally and openly, and they should be there after the death has occurred to answer questions. This open flow of information is essential if children are to go through life with a healthy attitude towards death.

It's hard enough for anyone, adult or child, to grasp the reality of the meaning of death when confronted with the death of someone close to them. Clear language does help to start the process, but it's hard to come to suddenly if it has never been part of the daily vocabulary. To use simple meaningful words with conviction when they're needed is not achieved without practice. If children haven't been talked to sincerely and warmly and lovingly about their dead pet, then it's going to be difficult to communicate with them about the death of someone important in their lives. If as children we have been unable to talk about death, as adults it's difficult to acquire the ability to do so. Linguistic evasiveness about death can all too easily spill over into our treatment of the dying person.

Children think logically and literally and they should be allowed to grieve in their own way. If they want to view the corpse they should be allowed to in a matter-of-fact, non-dramatic way. It's better not to encourage kissing, because the corpse is no longer the person they remember and is unexpectedly cold and marble-like. It's good for children to attend the funeral, especially if they can be taken step by step through the ceremony, and they should be given the freedom to visit the grave within the few days and weeks after the funeral, if they so wish. It's even more important for a child than for an adult to sit in on the "wake" chat and it's very reassuring to get the chance to talk and to hear about the dead person.

Grief shouldn't and mustn't be compromised for the sake of a partner – a woman, more than a man, will need to grieve for a lost foetus, or a stillborn child. It must also be remembered that the youngest child in a family, up to the arrival of the new baby, has enjoyed a special status in the family. Occasionally the child can develop decidedly homicidal tendencies towards the new baby. If anything does happen, such as a cot death, it's likely the older child will think that his death wish has been granted. In the case of a cot death, it's quite natural for a couple to blame each other for the death of their baby. Grandparents of a baby who dies can be unconsciously cruel to the baby's parents. This lashing out usually occurs because their natural reaction is that it is one of them who should have died rather than their grandchild.

* * *

The walk, it has been said, is as much in the raising of the foot as in the laying of it down, and death is as much a part of life as birth. As resurrection is central to Christian belief, death has always been part of the Church's dialogue. Sadly, in this era of instant communication and technological advances, we've become so frightened of the whole area of death that we've allowed the bereaved to become distanced from us. Even more sadly, we've allowed ourselves to become powerless because we've forgotten that our essential power is rooted in basic manifestations, such as being there, being real, being honest and allowing the bereaved to be the same.

Decreased awareness of the dying process has resulted in an increased preoccupation with fantasy at the expense of fact. Several different factors conspire to "forbid" death in our own culture.

It is glibly argued that the attempt to hide the truth

from the dying by the living is both for the sake of the dying and for the sake of society. We've reached such a point of so-called civilisation today that for too many people expressions of distress or despair are painful to witness.

A further reaction to the denial of death and the ignoring of grief, widespread in the first half of this century, has been an increased interest in bereavement. The behaviour associated with grief is influenced by the processes occurring during bereavement. These include the attempt to avoid or to deny the loss and the need to search for the dead person. The gradual acceptance of the absence of the loved one will wax and wane in importance as time progresses.

The improved technology available to doctors has resulted in an alteration in our perception of death. It is widely felt that medical people, rather than the clergy, are the appropriate presidents of the dying process. This has coincided with a decline in public religious practice, while at the same time, improved public health and scientific medicine have increased public expectation of longevity. The result is that doctors, even in the terminal care field, are seen by the dying as their hope of cure. Contemporary medical training, with its emphasis on high-technology curative medicine, ill-equips most doctors for maintaining hope while bodily function degenerates. This professional denial further "forbids" death. A decline in infant mortality and increased longevity have made the experience of caring for the dying more unusual in our culture than it was fifty years ago. This has been accentuated by the increased tendency for death to take place in hospital.

This medicalisation of death increases the dependence of the living on high-technology medicine. Sadly, it seems that for our generation, the concept of natural death has been ousted by the medicalisation of the struggle against death.

5

BLESSED ARE THEY THAT MOURN

A dictionary definition of grief is "great mourning, sorrow, affliction", and William Shakespeare goes so far as to call it "bodily pain". The manifestations of grief range from a momentary response right through to a total breakdown in function requiring admission to hospital.

"Grief-shot" is the phrase Maude uses to describe her own feelings after the death of her partner. She and Neil had been together for ten years. Both were in the theatre and their lives were inextricably bound to each other. For years Maude has maintained that her mourning of Neil was more intense, more grief-ridden than any other bereavement. It took her many sessions of counselling to realise and to accept that her mourning had taken a classic form and was extremely healthy.

Interestingly, when most people come to dying, they're reminded of all the things they may have grieved for or failed to grieve for during their lives. While grief is entirely subjective, the generally recognised stages of normal grief are: numbness and disbelief; acute grief; depression and despair; resolution. While these usually describe the grief related to bereavement, they can also apply to the grief which occurs at the time of a terminal diagnosis and even, indeed, when a relationship breaks up. Reaction to grief is very individual. Not everyone's grieving follows the "classic" pattern and different reactions can come and go and vary in duration.

Numbness and disbelief
Numbness and disbelief are protective functions, allowing the person to absorb the full impact of the situtation over a period of time. What has happened is accepted intellectually, but there's a paralysis of feeling. Numbness is a common reaction in the first few hours or days when the newly bereaved just can't believe their loss and may even recognise themselves that the truth hasn't yet sunk in. During this stage, the bereaved person may seem composed and, on a superficial level, appear to be coping very well.

Orla's story
When Dermot and Orla were told that Orla had Motor Neuron Disease (MND), their devastation initially manifested itself in numbness. Although MND occurs with around the same frequency as Multiple Sclerosis (MS), the fatality rate is much higher, as few patients live longer than five years. At any time there are only about two hundred people in Ireland with the disease and the result is that it doesn't have a very high profile, nor is there much public awareness of it. About eighty per cent of MND sufferers in Ireland have to be nursed at home, as there is little other option. British physicist Stephen Hawking, regarded by many as the Einstein of the era, who has had MND for twenty-eight years, is an exception. Actor David Niven also succumbed to the disease. As is often the case, many people attributed his initial symptom of slurred speech to alcohol.

In the beginning Dermot and Orla didn't seem to take in the fact that it was likely that she would be dead within five years, during which time her ability to move, swallow, chew and talk would gradually cease to function. She was only thirty-five years of age and the couple had four children ranging in age from seventeen to ten.

Motor Neuron Disease was first discovered in the 1850s. It is caused by the degeneration of the motor neurons, resulting in weakness, stiffness and resistance to movement, as well as muscle wasting, weakness, flickering and cramps. The majority of people with MND are over fifty years of age and there is a male predominance of 2:1.

MND presents itself in various ways depending on which particular groups of muscle fibres degenerate initially. In Orla's case, her first symptom was a "dropped" foot and Dermot remembers well the day she first knew she had to face up to something being seriously wrong. "She got out of the car and stumbled. Her leg just didn't seem to function, and she said she supposed she'd better see our doctor, as she'd noticed her hand and leg movements becoming awkward". Gradually, the deterioration of the "fine" movement in her right hand occurred and she had difficulty writing, but not holding a cup.

Orla's deterioration was rapid. The muscles of her tongue and swallowing mechanism became affected, her speech slurred and she had difficulty swallowing and coughing. Within months she was wheelchair-bound, but still hoping for a miracle. "In the beginning I was numb. I just couldn't accept what was happening to me. My body seemed to be disintegrating and yet my mind was very sharp. Dermot and I didn't discuss that I was going to die. The children were either creeping around the place or behaving appallingly. We were living a pretend existence. We had family and friends helping out and they seemed more embarrassed than anything".

Gradually Orla began to accept her disease, to acknowledge that she would die and to talk about it with her family. Together they defused a lot of anger and did a lot of crying, but their acceptance made the last months of Orla's life rewarding. She was assessed in the Central Remedial Clinic, which has the largest and most up-to-date micro-electronic resource centre in Ireland, and learned to communicate by means of a computer. Towards the end of her life, she required round-the-clock nursing and, although she only had movement in her left knee, she still managed to use the computer to keep in touch and to make contact up to three days before her death. She died peacefully at home, of respiratory failure, surrounded by her family.

Acute grief
Acute grief encompasses searching, anger, anxiety, restlessness and pining. It is the evocation of powerful fundamental responses which are part of our biological equipment for survival. When somebody close to us dies, we often have the urge to cry out loudly, bewailing, lamenting. This is a reaction dating back to primitive times, which invites others to share in our distress. It also brings the relief that accompanies the expression of powerful emotion. Where noisy lamentation isn't possible and this urge has to be restrained, the bereaved can end up burning inside and wearing the haggard expression of silent grief. This is one of the reasons why wakes, with their loud lamentations, were of such benefit. Today, acute grief is best seen in the way the travelling people mourn their dead. They are

immediately into a primitive lamentation that calls for screaming, shouting and even roaring. This helps to move grief forward and enables the bereaved, in most cases, to pick up the threads of their life again sooner rather than later.

When Paula's brother Robert died suddenly of a heart attack while holidaying with her family, she was devastated, but reckoned she was the one who had to remain "strong". She organised the removal, funeral and lunch back in her house for relatives. Robert's wife and children and her mother were the chief mourners. They received a lot of sympathy and comfort and were encourged both to weep and to reminisce. Paula took a back place and in so doing deferred her own natural mourning process. A year later she was still unable to pick up the threads of her life. It was only when she went to Robert's grave that the enormity of her loss hit her. In the quiet graveyard, the tears began to flow and she threw back her head and howled long and hard. Afterwards she said that she had never felt so lonely, isolated or desolate in her life. She desperately wanted someone to comfort her, but she'd come alone.

Also part of the acute grief syndrome are searching and anger. It's not unusual for bereaved people to try to find the person who has died. They know that their behaviour isn't rational, yet they repeatedly go to the grave, to the deceased's room or other places where they feel their loved one might be found. Constant dis-appointment can lead to a sense of outrage – the feeling of being robbed of someone precious – and the feeling that much of what was hoped for in the future is sud-denly gone. Regretfully in the "controlled" times we live in, post-bereavement anger, like loud lamentation, is often regarded as unacceptable and too many bereaved people have to hide it.

People often displace their anger onto those around them. They become irritable with their family and with anyone who wants to help them. Jennifer knows only too well that trying to comfort the bereaved can be a seemingly thankless task. When her aunt died she was her uncle's only close relative living nearby. With the best will in the world, she tried to take him under her and her family's protective wing. It took months for her to realise that the reason he was so angry and bitter was that he only wanted the return of his wife and that Jennifer had no consolation to offer. Once she could accept this she was able to understand her uncle's behaviour and his anger gradually dissipated. If the situation hadn't been handled so sensitively, he could easily have withdrawn, become alienated and lonely and begun to think that no one cared for him. He'd have felt neglected by his niece, would have been neglected as a result of his withdrawal, and anger about this would have been added to his grief.

Rory always regarded himself as religious. When his wife died he blamed God personally, not only for her death, but also for her manner of dying. He spent several weeks being very angry, and lost his faith for a few months. He tried to isolate himself from friends and from clergy, but recognising that his attitude was a normal part of the grief process, they kept in touch. It's quite usual for bereaved people, who are more religious than most, to suffer a temporary loss of their accustomed sense of the presence of God, and of their ability to pray. This adds to their distress.

Another unnerving part of the acute grief phase is

the very real physical sensations and responses. These can be all-consuming, due to over-activity of the autonomic nervous system. Breathing takes the form of deep sighs; appetite is lost and the bowel function is disturbed, resulting in diarrhoea while anxiety is most prominent, and constipation later when depression supervenes. Other digestive upsets are common, and if the deceased had a gastro-intestinal complaint, the bereaved may begin to experience similar symptoms, especially as some weight loss is common after the death of a loved one. Similarly, the palpitations that often accompany anxiety may be misinterpreted as evidence of heart disease, especially if it was the cause of the patient's death. Insomnia is usual, with restlessness both day and night, followed, in the more depressed phase, by feelings of overwhelming fatigue. Particularly if the patient was nursed at home and the relatives have been on call for many days and nights, their vigilance does not cease with the death. They sleep fitfully and in their dreams may think they hear the patient calling them.

To come to terms with the death of a loved one, many bereaved people rationalise, mentally regurgitating the events leading up to the death. There's the memory of instances where things might have been done or said differently, the hurts to be remembered, the joys to be savoured, the wondering how much they're to blame for the death. This makes the death real: allows it to sink in. When anger and blame are turned on to ourselves, they lead to guilt – a common and healthy part of grief. When none of these things happens, and anger is suppressed, depression or psychosomatic illness may occur later on.

Anxiety, an alarm reaction to loss of an attachment figure, is another feature of acute grief. It's tied up with the insecurity produced by the disruption of customary patterns of activity. Most of us take for granted many of the sequences of everyday life where a given stimulus provokes a given response. When it doesn't happen we are, at the very least, thrown out of sync. A very simple example is the death of a dog. For many years the ring of the doorbell is followed by an enthusiastic barking. When the dog dies, the ring is followed by a loud silence, reminding us again and again that the dog is dead.

Eileen had compassionate leave and took a few more days owing to her after her mother died. She reckons it was a foolish decision. So many little things reminded her of her mother. "I was regularly stopped in my tracks by the impact of her death. I felt lost and exhausted. I'd always thought I was very independent, but so many of the things I was used to doing were initiated by mum", says Eileen. "I got up early in the morning to make her a cup of tea and buy the newspaper before I left for the office. On Saturdays we did the weekly shopping and she'd get her hair done. Suddenly she was no longer there."

The routine of Eileen's life had broken down and she became purposelessly agitated for a few days. This was replaced by being miserably inactive, until with time, a new routine emerged. Eileen's agitation was partly as a result of conflict between the urge to search for her mother and the opposite one of wanting to avoid the pain. The vicious circle that ensues accounts for the restlessness of grief, with its attendant inability to settle down to doing anything constructive.

As the reality of the loss sinks in, pining begins. Eileen experienced a totally out-of-character longing to have her mother back. She became preoccupied with thoughts of her and was almost overwhelmed with waves of sorrow – the so-called pangs of grief. These lasted from a few minutes to an hour and returned several times during the day, especially when offers of sympathy or certain events served as reminders of her mother's death. They were intense and frequent for the first week or two and then began to subside gradually.

An awareness of the presence of the deceased is common in the early stages of grief and is an attempt by the psyche to mitigate the sense of loss. May really felt her mother with her. She could actually smell her perfume and on occasions when she went into the lounge, she seemed to be sitting in her favourite armchair. May found this sense of presence comforting, and held long animated conversations with her mother. Less than a week after her funeral, she decided to redecorate the room that had been Nancy's. "It sounds daft, but I even consulted her about the colours. The strange thing is that several months later it's still more her room than ours."

Hearing the deceased's voice, their footsteps, a waft of their perfume or aftershave or momentarily mistaking a face in the crowd for theirs is a normal part of the grieving process. These pseudo-manifestations are usually followed by disappointment as the realisation dawns that the person is dead. True hallucinations can occur too and are not a sign of impending insanity.

Taking on attitudes and mannerisms of the deceased is a way of trying to make sure that the loved one is kept alive in the mind. When Jennifer's aunt was alive, she always kept a light burning before the statue of the Sacred Heart. Over the years Jennifer had heard her uncle muttering about it often enough to realise it was a tradition that he'd little time for. Yet once her aunt had died, keeping the lamp burning became an important and integral part of his daily routine.

Gradually the symptoms of acute grief begin to give way. The rituals of the funeral have started the process. The mere fact of having to live continues it. Disposing of the deceased's possessions and dealing with the unfinished business all help the bereaved person to accept that the deceased has really gone. With time, anxiety and the pangs of grief become less prominent and their place is taken by the depression and despair which characterise mourning.

Depression and despair
The actual realisation and acceptance of death can lead to depression, but much of the depression in bereavement is a necessary trough. The bereaved person's space shouldn't be invaded, nor should well-meaning relatives seek to drag them out of it. It's a catch-22 situation that requires delicate handling, because if a bereaved person is left alone too much, that desertion can lead to isolation; if days are too filled with activity, the grieving process will be deferred.

It is the casual callers who are so important to the newly bereaved – the ones who make and keep contact. When Catherine's husband, Kevin, died suddenly in an accident leaving her with four small children, many of their friends were as shocked as she was. For the first time, with the death of one of their contemporaries, that group had to face their own mortality. The ones it scared shied away from Catherine, as though her bad luck would rub off on them.

"I went through a terrible stage after Kevin died. I just functioned for the children and was totally numb. The people we used to socialise with on Saturday nights continued to ask me out, but I just couldn't bear it because I missed Kevin horribly. It was really a case of everyone being able to master a grief, except he that has it. I remember one day somebody I hadn't seen for years just arrived at the door. She had always been more of an acquaintance than a friend. She had a quiche and a bottle of wine and said she hoped we could have lunch together. I thought maybe she hadn't heard about Kevin, but she had. And she asked a whole lot of questions about him. I found myself talking in a way I hadn't been able to with any of our really close mutual friends."

Catherine isn't the only bereaved person to need a cord to link her to the outside. The death of a loved one isn't got over easily. Once the initial sharp grief had passed, Catherine felt she should be coming out of the mourning syndrome. She regularly added up the pluses in her life. They included four healthy children, a fine house, a circle of caring relatives and friends and last, but not least, no financial worries. She was feeling hopeless and apathetic, without a sense of purpose and was carrying out the essential routines of living with no interest or pleasure. Withdrawal from others is quite usual, especally if they're reminders of the prospect of change.

Subconsciously Catherine was grateful for the attention and reassurance she received, but she reckoned it really didn't help her. Sometimes she wanted to scream at the people who called and telephoned to leave her alone. It was only years later that she could appreciate the patience shown her, the people who kept her company without pushing, until they saw the first sign about nine months after Kevin's death that she was beginning to recover. One day, to her surprise, she began to feel better. She was genuinely pleased to accept an invitation out, for herself, not for the sake of the person who'd invited her. The following week she bought a new blouse. Her grief was coming to an end and she was now on the way to gaining a new identity and life-style.

During this stage it is not unusual for the bereaved to become preoccupied with the dead person. This can be associated with searching behaviour and protest and, although it may appear bizarre, it is entirely normal. Out of sight is not out of mind. It was important for Catherine to keep Kevin's possessions in sight so that she and the children could readily bring him to mind for grieving purposes.

When John's wife died, family and friends encouraged him to get rid of her clothes. It took him six months before he could bear to part with even one pair of her shoes. He lived alone and, although he held down a demanding job, he was reminded of his wife's absence every night when he returned from the office. After eating a solitary meal, it gave him great comfort to go up to the bedroom they'd shared for twenty years, open her side of the wardrobe and finger her clothes, remembering the different occasions when she'd worn them. There came a time one night when, after finishing his dinner, he turned on the television, sat back and enjoyed a film. The next day he made plans to dispose of most of his wife's clothes. Seven years later, he still has a few selected items. There are still occasions when he needs their solace.

Resolution

Acceptance is all about learning to live well with the new reality. To be worthwhile, life must pick up and, indeed, embrace wholeheartedly, the essential pieces. Acceptance is saying yes to life and love, taking it one day at a time, being true to the whole range of feelings that make us human, going with the ups and downs of life, with the joys and the sorrows of living. After acceptance there's participation and that's all about taking up the threads of life again in a rewarding and fulfilling way.

Professional bereavement counsellors recognise that one of the healthiest grieving therapies of all is the photograph album. Turning its pages and re-living its pictures, particularly with family or close friends, is healing in itself. It is of even greater benefit if it is done with a close friend who is at ease with the death.

Resolution of grief is associated with the establishment of a new identity, incorporating the loss, but managing to form new relationships again. There are no hard and fast rules, nor time span. The experience of grief is subjective and everyone copes with it differently. This resolution may happen within the first two years, although for many, it progresses through a series of achievements beginning after the first few months. These tasks might include dealing with clothes, rearranging the bedroom, revisiting significant places and entertaining friends.

Bereavement counselling

Because of the times we live in, our attitude to dying and death and our general lack of support and understanding for the bereaved, many people who are unable to work through their grief alone can find support and strength in bereavement counselling.

Joy's mother had been ill with several minor complaints for a long time, and was slowly deteriorating. As Joy left the house before 8 a.m. each weekday, she knew that sooner or later she'd have to make arrangements to have her mother cared for professionally. In the meantime, she had a series of friends who looked in throughout the day. Her mother started vomiting suddenly one Saturday night while they were watching television. The ambulance was called, and within half an hour her mother was in hospital. As Joy suspected, it was her heart, and she was told by the overworked doctor in a matter-of-fact manner that her mother would probably die within twenty-four hours. She died within twelve hours of admission and Joy was so rushed alerting relatives, making funeral arrangements and entertaining the steady stream of people who called to the house that she had no time to grieve herself.

After the funeral, she took a few days off, but was so unsettled that she found it easier to return to the office than to face her feelings. Friends were supportive up to the time of the burial, but after that they wanted to get on with their own lives and expected her to do the same. She kept reminding herself of how lucky she was to have been at home when her mother was taken ill; she knew she had made her mother feel happy and productive during her last years and that she had nothing to reproach herself with, but she still felt terrible.

One morning, while reading the paper and drinking a cup of coffee before settling down to work, she saw an ad for bereavement counselling. She went for one session only, talked her heart out and, in her own words, "has never looked back".

The Hospice Foundation Bereavement Support Service was established in March 1987 under the Hospice umbrella to fulfil the need of bereaved people for an outlet for and acceptance of their grief. During the first years, there was an attendance of eight to ten people at the monthly meetings. Since then a large number of volunteers have completed the training course and many more are currently in training. While the majority of trained volunteers continue to work in the Support Service, some have gone on to develop and/or to contribute to bereavement services in other parts of the country, or are using their training in their own professional work with the dying and their families.

Since its inception, the bereavement service in Harold's Cross has expanded from one meeting to several meetings a month and attendance has increased enormously. At these meetings the bereaved and their families and/or friends meet a member of the support group on an individual basis. Once a month a short talk is given which is followed by a discussion at which the bereaved find it helpful to share their experience of loss with another person. Some come to meetings alone, others bring families or friends. Some come regularly, others on one occasion only.

Like hospices, bereavement counselling groups have sprung up throughout the country and are increasingly well attended. The best way of making contact with a group is through local clergy, hospital or health board.

6

SUFFER THE LITTLE CHILDREN

The death of a child is particularly poignant, because children haven't lived their natural life span and have been cut off in mid-flight. The sadness for parents, grandparents and the extended family can be all-consuming and the phrase "waste of a life" is used repeatedly.

Katy's story
Katy was ten when she died of cystic fibrosis. "It's only as the months pass that I realise how much I needed that time at home with her while she was dying. It made it possible for me to accept fully that she had to die", says her father, Jack. "It also gave all of us a chance to do what was left to be done for her – to make her comfortable, to provide her with familiar things and, most important, to surround her with the love of family and friends. We too were surrounded. We could never have nursed Katy at home without the love and help of so many people."

Katy had lived in the shadow of death since she was diagnosed as having cystic fibrosis at the age of three months. It is a genetically inherited disease affecting the lungs and digestive system, and both parents have to be carriers. The other two children in the family have not been affected. Katy's parents wanted her to spend as much time at home as possible, but nursing her wasn't easy. As is the case with many children who have cystic fibrosis, Katy was warm, intelligent, funny and determined to live her puny life to the full. She was buried in her favourite outfit, a red tutu and ballet shoes.

"She was constantly on antibiotics and the digestive disorder which goes with cystic fibrosis necessitated taking artificial enzymes", says her mother Margaret. "She suffered from lack of energy and breathlessness and had a constant cough." Katy's parents' attitude and their acceptance of her limitations and subsequent death owes much to their deeply spiritual beliefs. Their sadness at their bereavement was in no way mixed with bitterness at their loss.

Jack never ruled out the possibility of her being cured. Margaret is more pragmatic. "For years I've known that God wanted Katy back sooner rather than later." Katy was in Lourdes on several occasions and her last respite from her symptoms occurred there just six months before her death. A month after that last pilgrimage, Katy was put on the active list for a heart and lung transplant in Harefield Hospital in Middlesex, but a donor wasn't found in time. "She often said that her cough would only go in heaven where she'd get a new body."

Katy's final deterioration started a month before she died. "We knew she'd be more comfortable at home, and we desperately wanted her with us, but if the hospital could have done anything to help her, we'd have been happy to have her there", says Margaret. During the days preceding her death, Katy was suffering from fluid retention and was on eight litres of oxygen per minute. Her only sustenance was a yoghurt drink and jelly sweets. "Her heart was beating excessively fast and her lungs and heart were battling it out for oxygen", says Jack. "She was racing to the finish, but I still didn't believe she was on the way out". At 3.00 on the morning of her death, Jack, exhausted, lay down for a few hours, leaving Margaret and her mother keeping vigil.

Margaret takes up the story. "Katy had no breath. I said to her, 'You'll be all right in the morning', and she was." Katy died at 5.00 am. Both her parents say that she knew death was imminent. "At the end she had a vision. Twice she called, 'Mummy, Mummy'. I believe our Lady was with her." When she was laid out, Jack says that he wouldn't have been surprised if Katy had sat up and said, "Let's have a cup of tea". It was only when the coffin was lowered into the grave with the resounding sound of the earth falling on wood that he really accepted the finality of his daughter's death.

Children's attitudes

Children differ greatly from adults in their understanding of the cause of illness, its treatment and prevention. Indeed, research carried out in the UK some years ago showed that some children believed that you went to hospital healthy and became ill there; others thought that people in hospitals always die; more have no idea of time in hospital, believing that admission lasts for years rather than days or weeks. There were those who believed that doctors or nurses set out deliberately to hurt them, a view which is held more strongly by children with a history of admissions than those who have had only brief hospital experiences. While nursing a child at home is best, there are many occasions when this is just not possible.

With the great advances in symptom control, pain, and the other distressing features associated with the terminal phase of illness, need no longer feature. That said, there is still much research to be done into paediatric pain control, as children's absorption of and response to drugs is different from that of adults. Despite the trauma of watching a child die, it is of great comfort for parents to know that their child is being relieved of suffering, even when its level of consciousness is such that he's not really aware of it. Research continues to confirm the importance of minimising symptoms. Many bereaved relatives are highly relieved at the effect of the drug hyoscine, which eliminates the "death rattle".

Caring for the physical needs of a sick and dying child can make all the difference between constant discomfort and nagging reminders and freeing the child to concentrate on positive and outgoing behaviour. Ideally and when possible, care of the skin, hair and teeth should help the child feel attractive and comfortable. Skin that's bathed and powdered or moisturised promotes a sense of well-being. Girls' hair can be tied up in pretty ribbons, or Alice-bands; even the toughest young fellows get a thrill out of the latest hairstyle. It's worth persevering with cleaning the teeth, despite the difficulties that this often presents with a fractious child.

There's a wonderful selection of inexpensive, comfortable, easy care, brightly coloured clothes on the market. Garments that are easy to get in and out of are readily available and the sick child should be encouraged to choose her outfit every day. Initially, when Jenny was confined to bed, she wore a pretty nightie with pastel blue sprigging, or pale pink striped pyjamas. Her mother never thought of suggesting an alternative.

When her aunt brought her purple leggings, a hot pink, wide-necked T-shirt with splatters of lime green and acid yellow socks, she fingered them wistfully and said she wished she could wear them. As her aunt told her, there was no reason why she couldn't and she did, adding more colours and enjoying the psychedelic effect. Jenny's clothes became quite a talking point.

To tempt a jaded and sick palate, diet needs to be as imaginative and as varied as possible. Little and often is better and less off-putting than the usual three regular meals a day. If the child can only tolerate fluids, there are many palatable milk-based drinks and a great variety of very pleasant fruit juices. The majority of bed-bound people suffer from constipation and children are no exception, but before using laxatives, the introduction of fibre into the diet, if possible, can loosen the bowels.

Keeping children amused can be a difficult exercise, even when they're in the full of their health; but keeping boredom at bay when a child is sick calls for a lot of ingenuity. The majority of children soak up knowledge like sponges and get a great sense of achievement from learning. If the child is well enough, educational toys, board games, painting (if you can stand the mess, though plastic sheeting works wonders), Playdoh etc. should all be introduced. Children are social beings who enjoy company, and even the most stimulating game takes on an added dimension if shared with parents, brothers and sisters or friends.

Tennyson wrote of music lying gentler on the spirit than tired eyelids upon tired eyes, and a background of music can work wonders for a sick child. Also, most children love poetry and having stories read out loud to them.

It's difficult to explain illness to children under the age of seven, as they have a very limited understanding of their bodies. Often they'll just about realise that they have a heart, brain, blood and bones inside them. Awareness of their function is also very simple – the heart is for loving and the brain is for doing sums. They often believe that illness is a punishment for bad behaviour or that it is some magical rite and that all illness is contagious. Understandably, they have no comprehension of how treatment can make them better – why should the swallowing of a substance or an injection in the leg make an arm feel better?

Between the ages of seven and eleven, children become more informed, but their views are often incorrect. They believe illness is caused by contact with germs; they still hold on to their younger ideas on contagion; they are suspicious of treatment and often believe that a return to normality is a relapse. By the age of eleven, they'll know they have a stomach for "storing food", and a few will be aware that food is converted to blood and waste; they'll know that they have a lung – usually just one – and that breathing is through the mouth.

From about the age of eleven onwards, children begin to understand the functions of the digestive, respiratory and circulatory systems within the body. They also accept the necessity of sometimes enduring short-term discomfort for a long-term cure.

Children's belief about illness and death is affected by individual experience – some become relatively mature in their understanding of their own disease; others are aware that their illness causes parental anxiety. The fact that parents and doctors tend not to keep children informed about illness can cause them more stress than if they were given their prognosis in a way that they could understand.

Several classic stories illustrate how adults and children can often be on different wavelengths. One of the best known is a doctor telling a child that he had diabetes. For weeks that child believed that he would "die of betes". Jane was six when her young brother Billy died and her mother felt she had done a comprehensive job of explaining death and burial. To her surprise, when visiting the grave some months later, Jane asked quite seriously after looking at the dates on the grave, "Is that Billy's telephone number?" Five-year-old Ian thought that people turn into statues when they die, owing to the fact that he first met Oliver Goldsmith in the grounds of Trinity College and was told that he had been dead for some time. Tales like these show how adults forget how difficult it is for children to understand death and its biological reality.

When Derek was diagnosed as having incurable leukaemia his parents vowed that there would be no secrets and that he and his two sisters would be told the truth about his condition in a way that would make Derek's living good and his ultimate death palatable. That their home became a haven of tranquillity and serenity during the next months was an added bonus. His parents also decided that they'd do their utmost to fulfil even a few of Derek's dreams. The whole family went to London to see the Christmas lights, took in a pantomime in the West End and got "after Christmas" presents in Hamleys. Every occasion and then every day was special as Derek's health deteriorated. There was open house and Derek's friends were encouraged to visit. When he died he was laid out at home on his parent's bed, which was covered with a new white quilt of which he'd approved, and there were white flowers and candles everywhere.

A year on Jack and Margaret have on several occasions directly experienced social embarrassment and its power to inhibit talk of death. As any parent who has experienced the death of a child knows, there's the dreaded question "And how many children do you have?" Margaret regularly talks about their "three children". She maintains that even though Katy is no longer alive, she is still their child. It's quite common for parents, particularly mothers, to give the number of children born to them, and to add, "but one died".

Ten years after the cot death of her four-month-old daughter, Karen, Judy explains that if out of consideration for her questioner she just lists the living children, she feels a deep sense of betrayal both to herself and to her dead child. "It's as though I'm denying her existence". Judy and Margaret find that the idea of replacing the dead person is the hardest advice they've been given. "It's as though the people believe that having had another child we've replaced Karen, but a human being cannot be replaced."

Cot deaths

A cot death or, to give it its technical name, sudden infant death (SID) is defined as "the sudden and unexpected death of a baby who has seemed well or almost well and whose death remains unexplained after the performance of a thorough post-mortem". Cot death is a diagnosis by exclusion. While these deaths can occur from birth to two years, ninety-seven per cent occur in babies under a year old; sixty per cent between two and four months and twenty-five per cent after six months. The ratio is two girls to three boys.

Cot deaths can happen anywhere, but usually in the home, be it in the cot, bed, car or pram, and about seventy per cent occur during the winter. Most babies die in their sleep, evenly divided between day and night – only about three per cent die while awake. Each year there are some twenty thousand cot deaths worldwide. In Ireland the incidence is 2.6 per 1,000 live births, making a total of between 160 and 170 per annum. It is not hereditary; recurrence within families is extremely rare, but often twins die or experience near sudden infant death on the same day. The incidence of SID is the same across all socio-economic groupings.

Sudden infant death is the third most common cause of infant death in any part of the world, closely following congenital abnormality and premature birth. Most of the normally formed babies who die in their first year of life suffer cot deaths. The causes are not known. Post-mortems may show evidence of mild infection, not sufficiently serious to cause death. Irish and international research has shown that cot deaths occur in breast-fed as well as bottle-fed babies. Cot deaths are not caused by suffocation, vomiting, choking, or allergic reactions to cows' milk.

Even though there are many opposing claims and theories about cot death, no one yet knows what causes it or how to prevent it. What researchers have recognised over the past thirty years is that it has no single cause. But when the practice of sleeping babies on their stomachs was changed to sleeping them on their back or sides, the cot death rate dropped by almost half. Why this is so is not clear, but it is thought to be related to overheating. ISIDA (Irish Sudden Infant Death Association) has a four-point advice plan which advocates:

- Sleeping a baby on his or her back or side
- Not allowing the baby to become too warm
- Not smoking during pregnancy and not allowing anyone to smoke near the baby during the first year of life
- Breastfeeding for the first few weeks, not because this in itself reduces the risk of cot death, but because it may reduce the risk of infection.

Karen's story

Judy will never forget the day Karen died. "It was a lovely day in the middle of September and I was going to walk over to my mother's with Karen for lunch before picking up the two boys from school." After breast-feeding her four-month-old daughter, Judy dressed her in a new outfit, duly admired her, gave her what was to be her last cuddle, placed her on her tummy in her pram and put her in the garden while she took a shower. The time was 12.45.

While she was putting on her make-up the doorbell rang. It was a school friend who'd been in Australia for the past six months. Judy revised her plans. They'd have lunch here. She opened a bottle of wine, and the two friends chatted while looking at the photos of Karen's christening. After a request "to see Karen in the flesh", Judy brought her in from the garden still in her pram.

"Her face looked grey and when I touched her cheek it was stone cold. I knew she was dead. I started screaming and shaking. I'm sorry I didn't lift her out and try to resuscitate her." Judy's friend brought Karen across the road to a nurse. They called the doctor and the priest and Karen was taken by ambulance to hospital. Judy wishes she'd gone with her.

She sat crying until her husband, Denis, got home. Their two sons, aged eight and five stood watching her, touched by the tragedy, but not understanding it. The parents had to go to hospital to complete formalities and to make identification. There they were encouraged to hold Karen. They didn't want to, but now they're so glad they did. After the post-mortem the death certificate stated that the cause of death was "sudden infant death syndrome". The evidence pointed towards Karen dying at 1.15 p.m. Both parents say they'd have liked a reason for Karen's death, that it would have helped them cope.

Karen's birth weight had been 8.5lbs. The following day one of her lungs congested and she was moved to intensive care. There the second lung collapsed. "When I brought her home, she was very contented and a great sleeper, but everyone commented on her wheeze and I was always getting her checked out."

"You don't expect to buy a family burial plot when you're thirty-four", adds Denis. But they're glad they didn't opt for the anonymity of the "Angels' corner". They do regret keeping the funeral private and going away the day after Karen was buried. Judy says, "When we came back friends and family who felt they were doing us a favour had removed every trace of Karen". Denis believes that "you can't jettison memories like that".

Judy and Denis agree that their close relationship helped them through the following months. They approached ISIDA and Judy says that when she talked to a befriender, she got hope and slowly began to realise that she too could learn to smile again. While Denis was happy with the counselling he got in hospital, he has benefited enormously from contact with other bereaved fathers in ISIDA. Yet Judy, Denis and their children had to work through their grief and they coped in different ways with the usual feelings of shock and anger. For months their eldest son feared that when he went to sleep he might die.

Against all advice, Judy and Denis decided to have another baby fairly quickly. Mary was born a month before Karen's first anniversary. There was more jubilation on her first birthday than when she was born. Her parents stress that "Mary is very much a person in her own right and in no way a replacement for Karen".

* * *

Acceptance of the death of their child has been an important factor in each of these parents' lives. They say they'll never be the same again, but the passage of time has brought them peace. Margaret and Jack maintain that it was easier for them, because they had time to get used to the fact that Katy would die. Judy and Denis believe that for them the suddenness of Karen's death was a long-term blessing in disguise.

Bart's story
A "sledgehammer blow" is the way Bill and Eleanor describe the death of their son, Bart. Six years on,

they're still having difficulty coming to terms with it. "After all he'd gone through and survived, his dying seems a mockery", says Eleanor. Bart had always had a gutsy enjoyment of life, but when he was fourteen and the school coach told him that with training and dedication he had a promising future in athletics, he was ecstatic.

The weekend before the Hallowe'en school break, Bart surpassed himself on the local track, but afterwards complained of a pain in his leg. His parents felt he'd been overdoing his training and suggested he take it easy for the next few days. A week later Bill brought him to their local GP, who examined him, found nothing amiss and wondered about stress. A fortnight later an X-ray pinpointed a tumour below the knee and while the family were still reeling from shock, the tumour was diagnosed malignant and amputation was suggested as the safest option. "Bart told us he'd prefer to be dead and we believed him. He wanted quality, not quantity of life", says Eleanor. "After a second opinion and much soul-searching, we decided to go for minor surgery, followed by radiation and chemotherapy."

Though a long, unpleasant procedure, the treatment was successful and there was great jubilation the day Bart received the all-clear. His parents were told that the drugs used in the chemotherapy had weakened his immune system, but that given time it would return to normal. Gradually the family relaxed, took up the threads of their life again and Bart began gentle training.

Bill and Eleanor went away for a long weekend, leaving Bart and his two older sisters at home. Then started one of those freak series of happenings that lack credibility in fiction, but do occur in life. When their grandfather suddenly took sick, the eldest, Janey, felt she should stay with him overnight, but her sister had received an unexpected invitation and was also away, which left Bart on his own and vociferously insistent that he could manage. In Bill and Eleanor's best interests, it was decided not to up-date them on the changes in family matters.

Before his parents went away, Bart had been disguising a sore throat. He mentioned it in passing in a group while they all got soaked at a rugby match, after which he went to his friend's house and watched a video until the shivers drove him home. Janey phoned next morning to say she wouldn't be back until late and when there was no reply, she presumed Bart had gone training. "Equally, when our call went unanswered, we weren't in the least worried", says Eleanor.

When Janey got home, Bart was in a coma and died soon after reaching hospital. Doctors told the family that his deterioration into pneumonia had been rapid, that he'd have known little about it and would have been unlikely to respond to drugs. Eleanor says that today her only comfort is her belief that Bart died unsuspectingly. "He'd been through so much that he was terrified of illness, hospitals and treatments. I'm glad he was spared that at the end."

7

WHEN DEATH IS CHOSEN

Suicide is an emotive subject which gives rise to widely diverging views: one school of thought maintains that competent adults have control over their lives and ought, therefore, to be able to choose the time and manner of death; at the other end of the spectrum there are those who believe that each moment of biological existence is of infinite value and that doctors are, therefore, required to maintain life for as long as possible. Every position between the two extremes has been debated long and hard.

Throughout history, the question of suicide has been discussed at great length and with great sophistication. Plato, Aristotle and the Stoics, the medieval Jewish and Christian thinkers, modern philosophers and writers like Donne, Hume, Kant and Nietzsche have all contributed to the debate. In *Good and Evil* Nietzsche said that "the thought of suicide is a great source of comfort: with it a calm passage is to be made across many a bad night".

Belief in the sanctity-of-life is widespread. While the specific definitions of it vary, all of them tend to reject any form of killing by private persons, the major exception being killing in self-defence. The sanctity-of-life rule of thumb crosses national boundaries and is also used internationally by those who believe in the concept as a basis for legislation on abortion, euthanasia and suicide.

The last two decades have seen a remarkable interest in rational suicide. Legislation which forbids it has come under critical re-examination in many countries – and this is at a time when medicine appears to have succeeded in prolonging life.

The word "suicide" has Latin roots, although there is no evidence of the existence of such a word in classical Latin. The conjunction of "sui" himself, and "caedere", to kill, is generally believed to be a seventeenth century formation. Interestingly, suicide isn't mentioned anywhere in the New Testament and St Augustine is usually credited with being the architect of Christian condemnation of suicide.

Suicide has many grey areas and it is often difficult to distinguish between suicide and accidental death. In Ireland suicide is still regarded as a criminal offence, although legislation to decriminalise it has been under active, but ineffective discussion for several years. Death by hanging is regarded as being one of the easiest to define as suicide, though the cause of death will be stated as "asphyxia due to hanging, probably self-inflicted". Taking poison, drowning, carbon monoxide poisoning or shooting can be accidental or suicidal.

Death, even when expected, is a shock to relatives. Sudden death is a traumatic experience and suicide carries with it so much trauma and social stigma that relatives consumed by shock and sorrow often don't realise that it is a criminal offence. For those who are left behind, suicide is the cruellest of deaths, and as it often occurs in the home, the reminders can be overwhelming.

A priest tells the story of an incident during the 1970s when he was a curate in Donegal. "I was taking Saturday night confessions when there was this commotion outside the box. It was the daughter of a family I visited regularly and she was in an awful state, saying her father had shot himself. I went up to the house and I will never forget the sight that met me in the kitchen. Joe had died of a shotgun wound and his brains were everywhere." Joe had been depressed since he'd learned that he had to have major surgery and he was intelligent enough to know that his prognosis was not good. Despite being given the benefit of the doubt that his death was accidental, local tongues wagged and eventually the family could take the innuendo no more and they left the area.

Josie's story

Josie's husband, Ted, had been dead only six months when her seventeen-year-old son, Neill, hanged himself in their garden. At both funerals she had seemed to cope and afterwards her friends said that she had "great acceptance". She talked quite freely, saying that she "felt easy" about Ted. She'd nursed him at home and said that she had come to accept the inevitability of his death weeks before he died.

In the immediate weeks after Neill's suicide, she did a lot of wondering if she'd allowed him enough involvement during Ted's final days and if she'd given him enough support afterwards. She became haunted by her inadequacy as a mother. During a late night telephone conversation with a friend, Paula, she said, "I drove out to the cliffs today and sat looking out to the sea. I decided that if I were Neill, I'd have gone into the sea and just kept swimming rather than hanging myself."

Paula was concerned, but Josie assured her that she was fine. They made an arrangement to have lunch in a week's time. Next day Josie went back to the cliff-top again. This time, while she sat and watched the sea, she put her hands around her throat, thumbs to the front, and squeezed as tightly as she could, and for a while she weighed up strangulation against drowning.

When she chatted to Paula that night, she spoke freely about her thoughts and passed the incident off laughingly. When her friend asked her if she had any serious thoughts of suicide, she was positively outraged. Next afternoon, she drove out to the cliffs again, drank most of a bottle of vodka, started up the engine and drove over the cliffs. She crashed on the rocks below and died on the way to hospital.

* * *

Studies carried out on suicide affirm that at some time between eighty and ninety per cent of people give suicide more than a passing thought. Currently, about twenty-five per cent of callers to the Dublin Samaritans express suicidal feelings. Suicidal thoughts can be triggered by grief and depression. Most people do not plan the details and usually consider suicide as an alternative to a difficult life situation.

For each "official" suicide in Ireland, expert opinion varies as to whether there are three or nine more. Before a death is logged as a suicide, information compiled from the inquest report, from the investigating gardai and from the media is taken into consideration. There are a lot of ifs and buts surrounding suicide and definite classification can be difficult, as well-inten-

tioned coronors and investigating gardai may be
tempted to conceal facts.

Traditionally Ireland has ranked low on the Euro-
pean scale of suicide, but since 1980 this has changed
and our suicide rate is coming into line with the
remainder of Europe. Currently more than one suicide
per day occurs in Ireland. The pattern of suicide in Ireland used to be that there were more rural than urban
suicides, but this is no longer the case. Despite the sta-
tistical grey area, it is known that the number of suicides is increasing and that a complete cross-section of
ages and socio-economic groups is affected. Over
recent years the number of young males committing
suicide has risen dramatically.

The Samaritans, who have been operating for nearly
fifty years, reckon that people show their suicidal feelings by:

- being withdrawn and unable to relate;
- having definite ideas of how to commit suicide, and
  maybe speaking of tidying up affairs, or giving
  other indications of planning suicide;
- talking about feeling isolated and lonely;
- expressing feelings of failure, uselessness, dispirit-
  edness, lack of hope or loss of self-esteem;
- constantly dwelling on problems for which there
  seems to be no solution;
- expressing the lack of a supporting philosophy of
  life such as religious belief.

The Samaritans have found the risk of suicide to be
greater where there is:

- recent loss or the break-up of a close relationship;

- current or anticipated unhappy change in health or circumstances, such as retirement or financial problems;
- painful and/or disabling physical illness;
- heavy use of or dependence on alcohol or other drugs;
- history of earlier suicidal behaviour;
- history of suicide in the family.

Paul's story

Paul was a successful businessman and a perfectionist at home. From the beginning he imbued his three children with the importance of succeeding. By the time they were young teenagers, they were completely alienated from him, and their mother, Eileen, trod a difficult path trying to keep some sort of harmony in the home.

When Paul's business went bankrupt, he told Eileen that he wished he were dead. It wasn't so much the money, but the fact that he had failed. "Initially I remember being hurt that he didn't confide in me that things were shaky. But then he never discussed the ins and outs of business at home – he thought my forte was more recipes than balance sheets. My first thought was that perhaps now we could become a normal family and when I said it to him he looked at me as though I had three heads and spoke about not letting standards slacken. He planned to build another business from the ground up and I dreaded it."

For six months Paul battled against the overall economic downturn, reluctant bankers and rising lending rates. Then one night he didn't come home for his dinner. Eileen rang the factory but there was no reply.

There was nowhere else to ring. Paul had no family and no friends. It was a state of affairs that he often spoke of proudly. In the small hours of the morning, Eileen was told by the police that her husband's car had been taken from the local river. He was in the driver's seat and was dead. "The more I think about it, the less surprised I am. Paul was consumed with the idea of failure, and with the way things were he was finding it very difficult to get another business off the ground. He just couldn't take it."

Eileen and her children grieved long and hard. She remembered his early kindness and tenderness and berated herself for not being able to keep them alive. She felt she'd failed as a wife and was diminished as a human being and was very much aware of the stigma it attached to her and her children. It took many sessions of counselling before she could come to terms with Paul's suicide, accept that it was not of her doing and look hopefully to the future. Her daughters grieved stormily, but her son retreated into himself. He'd never really known his father and now, at the age of fifteen, he realised that he'd never have the opportunity. Also, he had never been left in any doubt that he was a disappointment to his father and he had to come to terms too with a sensation of failure.

* * *

Much research on suicide has been carried out internationally but few definite conclusions have emerged concerning patterns of age, ethnic group, social status etc., although it seems obvious that the suicide rate increases as civilisation advances. Generally, suicide is more likely among men than women, but vice versa for attempted suicides; the suicide rate increases with age and is higher among the highest, rather than the lowest, income groups. Marital status and suicide are strictly interrelated. Divorced men and women have a higher suicide rate than the undivorced, and divorced women commit suicide less frequently than divorced men. Among the widowed, there is a high rate where the marriage was childless.

Though initially published in the early 1900s, French sociologist Emile Durkheim's *Le Suicide* is still regarded internationally as the bible on the subject. Since then, the chief advances in knowledge have come from statistics and psychoanalytic psychiatry. By studying religious affiliation, marriage and the family, and political and national communities, and then relating currents of suicide to social concomitants, Durkheim came up with three classifications of suicide: **egoistic**, resulting from lack of integration of the individual into society; **anomic**, where there is a lack of regulation of the individual by society and **altruistic**, where the individual's life is too rigorously governed by custom and habit. Durkheim believed that religion, or lack of it, played a vital role in the suicide stakes. He ascribed the comparative immunity of Catholics to suicide to the way in which they're integrated into a group with commonly-held sentiments and beliefs. These, he believed, relieved the individual of guilt, made sins forgivable and established an intricate hierarchical system of parental substitutes. Today, this is no longer relevant as many people who profess to be Catholic only pay lip service to religion.

Attempted suicide

While the figures for suicide are rising, attempted suicide is endemic. In the UK alone an estimated 100,000 people are admitted to hospital each year after deliberately taking drug overdoses or injuring themselves. While such figures are not available in Ireland, there is no reason to suppose that the situation here differs substantially, as attempted suicide is prevalent throughout the western world. Apart from the load this problem places on medical and psychiatric staff, it also has considerable impact on the work of GPs and social workers.

Attempted suicide is not necessarily regarded by the medical profession as a "disease", nor are those who attempt suicide necessarily seen as being "ill". Some people who attempt suicide may suffer serious physical harm or even die, and a certain proportion of them do have psychiatric disorders, but generally they're regarded as people made vulnerable by personal and social difficulties, but who are still responsible for their actions.

Most research concerning the problem of deliberate self-poisoning and self-injury has been based on patients referred to general hospitals, but the phenomenon occurs more widely than this method of detection suggests. A recent survey of general practitioners in Edinburgh indicated that they might be seeing as many as thirty per cent more cases than those referred to hospital. An investigation in Canada showed that more than two-thirds of the attempted suicide cases identified were not referred to a general hospital.

In the UK approximately nine out of ten cases of attempted suicide referred to general hospitals involve self-poisoning, the remainder self-injury, or self-poisoning and self-injury combined. For middle-aged people, most overdoses involve prescribed drugs, with minor tranquilizers and sedatives being the most commonly used. Analgesics, such as aspirin and paracetamol, are used more often by young people, especially adolescents, who joke that twelve paracetamols will "do the job of self-annihilation". They will, as there is no antidote and such a dose causes irreversible kidney failure with death usually occurring within two days. Other substances used for overdosing include anti-convulsant drugs, antibiotics and even disinfectants and turpentine.

The most common form of deliberate self-injury involves self-cutting, particularly of the wrists and arms. Wrist-cutting, predominantly a behaviour pattern of the young and an often-repeated act, is usually carried out in a state of detachment and may be motivated by the need to alleviate tension. (Self-mutilators usually suffer from serious personality disorders.) Other forms of self-injury, such as shooting, drowning, and jumping from heights, tend to involve older people. Severe intoxication with alcohol may in some cases be regarded as deliberate self-poisoning and alcohol is often consumed before a suicide attempt.

Recent studies carried out in the UK confirm that ninety per cent of people who committed suicide suffered from a recognised mental illness. Chronic suicide repeaters represent a relatively small proportion of the total attempted suicide population, but repetition increases the chances that they will subsequently succeed in killing themselves. There's a positive association between the number of attempts made and the provision of psychiatric treatment.

The reasons why people repeatedly take overdoses or inflict self-injuries are often unclear and this makes the task of helping them difficult. Some people lack the necessary life-coping resources; others may be unable to deal with tension; a few obtain excitement from the risk.

Teenage suicides

While there have been reports from the United States of attempted suicides in children under five years of age, these appear to be isolated cases. However, after the age of twelve, attempted suicide becomes increasingly common. Reasons put forward for this are that serious impulses towards suicidal behaviour don't occur until the development of the concept of death in late child-hood; that depression in children is rare; that children are closely integrated within the family; that despair and helplessness are not usually part of childhood.

Throughout the western world, teenage suicides are on the increase and Ireland is no exception. A survey was carried out in 1989 on suicidal behaviour in children in a disadvantaged urban area of Dublin by a psychoanalyst and child psychiatrist. The survey showed that fifteen per cent of the eighty boys surveyed, who were in the 9-11 age group, thought that life was not worth living most of the time and did have thoughts of killing themselves. In three out of the four children who tried to kill themselves, a family member had also attempted suicide.

Adolescent suicides in Ireland follow the international trend in that attempted suicide occurs more frequently in females than males, while suicides that succeed occur more frequently in males. Also, the more violent methods, such as hanging, are becoming increasingly common. The concern here about imitation is backed by evidence from the United States which shows that after television programmes in which a teenager attempts suicide, there is some increase in the suicide rate.

The increase in adolescent suicide over recent years is attributed to a build-up of stress in the home, at school and in relationships. When too much stress accumulates, something has to give and sadly, too often, the decision is to end life. The experts have no ready solution either, but they do say that "very distressing thoughts" are not uncommon among children and that it's important for both parents and teachers to create a climate for discussion.

Jane's story

Jane was a good student, but was always quiet at school and kept herself to herself. After she was orphaned at the age of eleven, she lived with her widowed aunt. She got a good Leaving Certificate at sixteen, topped the class in a commercial course and got a job in an insurance company. One of the panel at her interview remembers Jane as having "an efficient air and being quietly confident. Unlike most of the other interviewees, she didn't seem in the least nervous". On her first day in the job, Jane was made feel very welcome, and received a lot of help and encouragement, which, as was her way, she accepted with apparent indifference. At 3.30 p.m. she left her desk, and when the office was closing at 5.00 p.m. it was discovered she

111

wasn't in the building, even though her handbag and coat were still there. She was found the next morning at the bottom of a cliff twenty miles away.

* * *

In the majority of cases, adolescents who commit suicide, or even attempt suicide, have considerable problems in their relationship with their parents and there is often poor communication between them. When Joanne and Herbert returned from holidays they found that their nineteen-year-old student son had hanged himself in their bedroom. Ronald had had a stormy passage through his teenage years, but his parents felt that that was in the past, and that he'd settled into third-level study. They were amazed to discover that his friends had considered him disturbed for several months and were actually avoiding his company.

Sixteen-year-old Susan came from a family of five. She had an older brother, who had recently become engaged and was a high achiever, and her sister of twelve was the pet of the family. Her father had a chronic heart condition and her mother protected him to such an extent that Susan felt she could not discuss even the most minor problems with him. She had become alienated from her mother, mainly because she disapproved of her new boyfriend, and they were rowing a lot. Susan herself was concerned as her school work seemed to be falling off despite the amount of time she spent studying. She considered that her parents overestimated her academic ability and she felt scared and alone.

On the day she committed suicide, she had been taking her end-of-term examination in English and Maths, but felt she had done badly. She had arranged to see her boyfriend secretly that evening, but her mother had listened in on the extension phone and accused her of lying when she said she was going to a film with a classmate. They rowed vociferously for a good hour. Then Susan went to her bedroom, wrote a note saying how much she loved her boyfriend, took an overdose of approximately thirty aspirins and cut both her wrists with a razor.

* * *

Suicide has a triple effect. In the first place, a close relative or friend has died. Secondly, there is the pain and shock of sudden death. On top of those, the fact of suicide, with its additional pain and regret, has to be dealt with. The pain lasts a long time, as the grief associated with suicide leaves many unresolved doubts. People who've been touched by suicide invariably report that their emotions become intensified to unbelievable and unbearable proportions; many deny the actual death and even more deny the method. Floods of feelings, such as shame, anger, guilt, love, self-pity, bewilderment, rejection and self-blame, are normal.

8

THE PRACTICALITIES

There are many practicalities that cannot be ignored and have to be looked after when a family member dies. The death certificate is the first document to be obtained. Would you know where to get it? While most people have probably paid PRSI all their lives, the majority don't know how to claim a social welfare pension; nor do they know what other social welfare benefits they're entitled to.

It makes life much easier for those left behind if tax can readily be sorted out. And what about the occupational pension? Do you know your entitlements under the dead person's occupational pension plan? Nowadays most people have a mortgage protection policy which automatically pays off the outstanding balance when the policy-holder dies, but this should be checked out. If there isn't one, will you be able to continue to meet the mortgage payments? Most people don't know that when they die, their spouse's tax free allowance is reduced by almost fifty per cent. Where are the life assurance policies kept? Is the car insurance in the deceased person's name only? The list is endless. What it all adds up to is that if affairs aren't in order the grieving family is left with a load of extra problems. Often the fact that a will hasn't been made is the final straw.

Making a will
All too often making a will is associated with dying. Picture the scene – the dramatic rush by the solicitor to

the death-bed of his client, who's barely hanging on to make his last will and testament. We've seen it in countless films, absorbed it on TV and read about it in novels galore. Making a will should be done as early in life as possible, yet a large proportion of people shy away from it. Young people believe passionately in their own immortality, while the older generation are often fearful that actually making a will might precipitate their own death.

In Ireland a testator must be over eighteen years of age, or married, or have been married. A will is merely a legal and binding document which sets out the way in which the deceased person's possessions are to be disposed. These items can range from a house and land down to personal items of jewellery and clothing. Making a will facilitates the quick settlement of the estate after death. It's a very personal document and should be kept in a safe place; a solicitor's office or a bank are usual.

The advantages of making a will include having your estate and belongings distributed as you wish, reducing confusion and arguments, and it also assists your executors in the administration of your estate. Another major advantage of making a will is that it can be used in efficient tax planning and can help reduce any inheritance tax for which your heirs might be liable. There's a lot of confusion about inheritance tax. Quite simply, when you die, the distribution of everything you own – house, car, household contents, savings, life assurance, farm or business – could give rise to inheritance tax. One of the features of this tax is that the liability falls on the recipient of the inheritance and the rate of tax is determined with reference to the total value of all gifts and inheritances received after 2 June 1982. By leaving assets to several beneficiaries, each with their own tax-free threshold, the effects of inheritance tax can often be minimised.

It is also important to understand that a surviving spouse to whom you're validly married under Irish law at the time of death has a legal right to a portion of your estate, notwithstanding the provisions of your will; and the court may also order that provision be made for your children.

Dying intestate, i.e. without making a will, causes many problems for the family and relatives of the deceased. Too many people assume that after death their possessions will automatically pass to their husband or wife. This is not necessarily so. The law has the right to decide how an intestate's possessions should be distributed. When a person dies without making a will, the immediate family and extended family may claim against the estate. It's not unknown for a widow, or indeed widower, to have to sell the house to pay off relations.

Intestate estates are dealt with under the rules of intestacy, laid down by the Succession Act 1965. In the context of making a will children and grandchildren include adopted children and any children born out of wedlock, but not stepchildren. If there are no children or grandchildren the estate goes to the surviving spouse. Where there is a spouse and children, grandchildren or other descendants, two-thirds of the estate goes to the spouse and the children get the remaining third. Where there are children, but no surviving spouse, the children take the whole estate. Where someone has neither a surviving spouse nor issue, their estate is distributed to their parents and more remote relatives.

Insurance

In reality, life assurance is really death assurance, an idea which goes back to Roman times. The same basic principle of pooling and sharing risk still governs the operation of most forms of pure life assurance today. In its simplest form, life assurance is a means by which adequate financial provision is made for family and dependants in the event of untimely death. It operates on the basis of pooling risk. Each policy holder pays a premium into the pool and out of this pool of money the life company pays out to the dependants of those policy holders who die.

Today's life assurance industry is sophisticated and wide-ranging, providing a comprehensive choice of savings and investment products. Operating on the principle of pooling risk, the premium paid each year into the "life assurance pool or fund" is based on the insurance company's assessment of life expectancy and each company has a set of standard premium rates for people in good health.

There are more than twenty life assurance companies competing with each other in the life assurance market in Ireland. Each offers a range of products with their own distinctive features both in relation to premium costs and benefits provided. It is a good idea to discuss, with your spouse, and your broker, which type of policy will be best for you.

Life assurance policy documents should be kept in a safe place. It's a legal contract and it may be needed by others in the event of the policy-holder's death.

Nursing

While none of the Irish health boards has a specific aid

scheme in operation for terminally-ill people being nursed at home, they are instrumental in organising public nursing, and home help if considered necessary. Information can be obtained by contacting the Board's local director of community care and each case is individually assessed and considered. There's a director of community care for approximately every 100,000 people, which means that most counties throughout Ireland have their own director, although Dublin's population warrants eight and Cork has three.

Referrals to avail of public nursing, which is without charge, come from GPs, hospitals and people just ringing in. A nurse from each district liaises with hospitals in the area and is kept informed of terminally-ill people who are leaving hospital to be cared for at home. At this stage she will meet next-of-kin and familiarise herself, or the nurse who'll be dealing with the patient, of any unusual circumstances or forms of nursing required. These nurses are only too aware of the difference between the patient being in hospital, backed by a full support service, and being cared for at home, which, without professional input can be an intimidating experience. While the public nursing service usually operates between 9.00 a.m. to 5.00 p.m. five days a week, there is room for flexibility to meet the needs of the community.

The nurse assesses the situation, offering support to both the patient and the carer, who is taught how to look after the patient's personal needs. Family members who bring a terminally-ill patient home from hospital are more than willing to look after this person totally and when death takes place, because of their input of caring, their grieving is less debilitating. The

Health Boards claim that the dying have a priority call on their services and that their policy is to make sure that the needs of the dying are met. In practical terms this may include the provision of equipment such as a hoist, commode or hospital bed.

The Irish Cancer Society offers a free home care service throughout the country to cancer patients. Information can be obtained from local hospitals or health centres. The nurses used are specially trained in symptom control and patient/family counselling. The Irish Cancer Society's night nursing service operates nationwide and provides a night nurse free of charge for up to five nights to families with a very ill cancer patient being nursed at home.

Voluntary Health Insurance (VHI) allows a modest daily sum for forty-two days in the subscription year for home nursing, but an appeal can be made for an additional allowance on the basis of somebody being terminal, and an *ex gratia* payment can be negotiated. There is also an out-patient allowance of £1,200 (in 1992) per subscription year. This takes into account GP's visits, X-rays, physiotherapy etc. Medical expenses which are not recoverable from VHI can be claimed against income tax.

After death
One of the first practical acts carried out after a death in the home is getting the doctor to sign the death certificate. This is usually just a matter of form, particularly if the deceased has been ill for some time. The death then has to be registered, a task which is usually carried out by the next-of-kin. The custom of relatives and friends

viewing and praying over the body is a long-established one. From time immemorial there has been an almost universal practice of washing the corpse. At the very least it would reflect badly on the immediate family if the corpse was not clean and presentable. Today these ablutions are increasingly less likely to be carried out by the immediate family. Sometimes a nurse will do it, at other times nuns, and often the undertaker will make the arrangements.

Closely related to viewing, is the touching of the corpse. This usually involves touching the corpse's brow – in some cases this takes the form of a kiss. Folklorists suggest that at the back of this custom lies the belief that a murdered corpse will bleed if touched by the murderer. Other less sinister explanations are that it prevents bad dreams; removes the fear of death; is an act of sympathy with the mourners; signifies that the toucher bore the deceased no grudge and that by contact, the toucher gains the dead person's strength. The main purpose of viewing and touching the dead person is to comfort those left behind and to assuage their grief.

It's interesting to note that the majority of postmortem customs are for the benefit of the deceased's family and friends. That being said, wakes were designed to ward off evil spirits; the ringing of bells was believed to disturb the atmosphere and to confuse evil spirits, possibly thwarting their designs on the escaping soul. Other customs of this kind include opening the windows to allow the soul an easy escape route; covering mirrors to prevent haunting; and the putting out of fires and stopping of clocks to signify death. There's an ambivalence about the custom of drawing the curtains and wearing mourning – some people maintain it protects from evil spirits; others that it's a symbol of grief; more that that it's an indication of the new status of the family.

Funerals

There's evidence of the existence of funerary customs from a very early stage in our history. A Neanderthal skull, dating from approximately 60,000 BC, surrounded by mammalian bones, with evidence of fire and with eight different types of flowers woven into the branches of a shrub, was discovered this century in northern Iraq. Another skull of a similar age, with the bones and hide of a bison adjacent to it, was found in a cave in south-west France. There is much evidence of food and drink being buried with the dead throughout the ages. In certain respects, our early ancestors indicated a need to keep their dead near them, but not too near, as burial finds were well away from the remains of everyday life. The practice in some cultures of the wives or servants of the dead chief being buried alive with him indicates a fear that the dead might return to haunt the living.

This awareness of the presence of the dead can often bring acceptance. Maisie visits her son's grave regularly and derives great comfort from doing so. One occasion stands out particularly in her memory. "The cemetery is about five miles away and on the second anniversary of Joe's death, I cycled over, because there was nobody around to drive me. It was all foggy and misty, just like an Alfred Hitchcock film. I was standing alone at the grave talking to him, the way I always do, when suddenly I felt his presence very strongly. I knew he was okay and that he was happy and, you know, I was glad he was dead and had constant peace. I'd always been disappointed that he hadn't ever come to me in my dreams. Everyone else had dreamt about him – all his friends and the rest of the family, but from that day on I never minded".

Jody and Catherine were glad they bought a burial plot when the hospital offered "to dispose of the body" of their stillborn baby. Because it wasn't obvious whether the baby was a boy or girl they called it Enda, got a little coffin and had a priest friend say prayers over the grave, with only the immediate family in attendance. Jody regrets that he didn't insist on being with his wife during the birth; and that neither of them saw their baby. The hospital staff advised against it, but Catherine did turn back one edge of the blanket and her abiding memory is of one perfectly formed foot. The family draw immense comfort from being able to visit the grave.

Today when people die at home, a relative usually contacts the undertaker direct. Very often family and extended family have been using the same firm for a few generations. Otherwise, the choice of funeral director can be made on personal recommendation or in as haphazard a fashion as selecting a name from the *Golden Pages*. Funeral directors pride themselves on taking over the practicalities of arranging the funeral from the time they're called in and, particularly in rural areas, they become intimates of the family for the days between death and burial and on rare occasions, for even longer.

A country undertaker tells how Tom's parents called in to make arrangements for his funeral. They didn't want the undertaker coming to the house, as they felt it would scare nineteen-year-old Tom, their only son, who was dying from cancer. A few days later Tom himself, a trainee chef and a rock music fan, arrived at the undertakers. He was wearing a red baseball cap to disguise his lack of hair and if you didn't look too closely at him, you'd think he was just any other teenager. He didn't want his parents to know he'd been in. He felt they'd be upset, but he knew he hadn't long to live and he wanted a particular piece of music to be played during his funeral Mass. It was an instrumental piece put together by the local rock group when he first became sick. A few weeks later Tom's wish was carried out. During the service, there wasn't a dry eye in the church, as his friends brought up to the altar tokens of what had been important to Tom during his life, such as the baseball cap, a cookery book and his guitar. "It was such an emotional occasion that all of us felt the mourning was being drawn out of the family", remembers the funeral director.

The services offered by funeral directors include putting the death notice in the national newspapers; purchasing the grave, if necessary (graves can't be bought in county council graveyards in advance of death); making arrangements for cremation, if required; organising the hearse, music, choice of readings, flowers, cars, etc. Some more enterprising and caring undertakers cover the post-funeral situation. Says one, "Traditionally we haven't been involved with the family after the burial, but many of us feel an aftercare service is becoming increasingly important". This includes contacting the family within a couple of weeks of the burial to check if they need assistance with acknowledgements, getting memoriam cards printed, organising a headstone, inscriptions, tidying up the grave, etc.

Following trends in the US and the UK, the increasingly popular pre-need service is also on the modern undertaker's agenda. This can be anything from a simple consultation and advice, to complete funeral arrangements including full payment. It is the experience of undertakers that where there's family openness, the vast majority of terminally-ill patients will confide their last wishes to a family member, who often liaises between the funeral director and the person about to die.

If required, the undertaker can also organise the washing and laying out of the remains. If the body is to remain at home, the bed is usually favoured over the coffin, as it provides a more natural setting. If a funeral parlour is to be the last resting place, and there's an increasing trend towards this, the body is removed by ambulance. Despite family and friends having the freedom and privacy to visit the deceased in the funeral home during opening hours, funeral directors are aware of the long-term psychological importance for the family of giving them plenty of time to bid a formal farewell before the remains leave home. Embalming is necessary if the funeral isn't taking place for around three to four days, and it is now a legal requirement if remains have to be shipped overseas. If remains are coming in from a country where embalming isn't carried out, the coffin has to be lined with zinc and sealed.

Today the trend is towards being buried in ordinary clothes. Men are inclined to be buried in suits; women in a favourite dress; and children in casual gear. The undertakers supply the shrouds, which are factory- or convent-made. The colours are blue and white and brown, although the latter is seldom used anymore.

There are many reasons for the rise in the popularity of funeral homes, which, somewhat surprisingly, are more popular in rural than in urban areas. Architecturally and size-wise, the layout of most modern houses is just not suitable for keeping a dead body; nor for round-the-clock "waking". Often by the time death claims the patient, the carer's ability to function has come to an end. In these recessionary times, many people consider the costs of "waking" too high. A funeral director explains that "the days of washing and plugging the body and hoping for the best are gone. Modern medicine works wonders before death, but after death there can be a sanitation problem, which may be distressing for the family if it isn't addressed. The current methods of preparing the body are more easily carried out here than at home. Occasionally we'll sanitise the body and return it home until burial."

Customs surrounding the final farewell vary from country to country and from locality to locality. In Dublin most mourners, other than the immediate family, bypass the funeral home and go to the church; in most other Irish cities, the majority of people attend the funeral home to say goodbye to the body there. North of Dundalk the custom is for bodies to be taken from their residence for burial.

Cremation

Cremation has been used as an alternative method of disposal of remains after death for many centuries. Today all Christian denominations, including the Catholic Church, allow cremation. It is favoured by

practically all eastern religious sects, except for Ortho-
dox Judaism and Islam, which forbid it. But it is only
since the early 1960s that the Catholic Church began to
modify its laws concerning cremation. The first document on the matter, issued by the Vatican on 8 May
1963, instructed the bishops to discourage cremation –
this has subsequently changed. The change in attitude
with regard to cremation is in keeping with a Church
which has always accepted that extraordinary circumstances may exist to justify cremation, for instance in
times of war or during epidemics. National custom
combined with a public need may have given the
Church no alternative but to allow the cremation of
bodies; also there can be public and private reasons for
cremation. The expense of a funeral is an important factor today and one which influences people in their
choice of burial or cremation. In general, cremation is
less expensive than burial. This is because the cost of
burial is affected by the price of the grave and the
labour, as well as the expense of transporting the
corpse and the mourners to a cemetery which may be a
long distance from the church where the funeral rites
have taken place. Other reasons for cremation are
hygiene; the fact that many people have a horror of
burial; and that others dread the slow process of
decomposition in the grave.

The number of cremations in the Republic of Ireland
confirms that the majority of Irish people opt for the
more traditional burial. Cremation is favoured more by
city dwellers than by people living in rural areas. The
Dublin-based Glasnevin Crematorium Company is the
only company in the Republic which carries out cremations. Until it was established in the 1980s, remains des-

tined for cremation had to be sent outside the country to crematoria in the North of Ireland and Britain. The crematorium in Glasnevin is the most modern in Europe and the service has been designed to ensure the minimum emotional upset to the bereaved.

The questions most frequently asked by people are: Is the body taken out of the casket before going into the kiln? It is not. How long is it before remains are cremated? All remains are cremated within twenty-four hours of receipt. What happens after incineration? The ashes are put into an urn or a casket of light metal or plastic material for disposal. The bereaved can have the ashes delivered to their home if they wish. If undelivered ashes are not collected within three months, they're returned to the undertaker. That some ashes are never collected by the relatives of the deceased is attributed to the finality of cremation.

During the early days of cremation in Ireland, the scattering of ashes was the most popular method of disposal. But many relatives learned to their cost the importance of having a place to grieve and to meditate. In Glasnevin, there's a choice between the columbarium (literally translated as "a niche for a dove") or burial of ashes in the garden of remembrance. In both cases a site can be reserved for the next of kin and this option is proving particularly popular in the garden. The traditional family grave is also often used as a final resting place for ashes. The crematorium staff recommend that if it is the wish of the deceased that ashes be scattered, that the living should hold on to some. Gemma's husband requested that his ashes be strewn at his favourite bathing spot, as he wanted his friends to know that he was always with them. She solved the problem by buying lockets for herself and each of her daughters into which she put a little of his ashes prior to carrying out his wishes.

There is nothing in the general laws of the Church about the disposal of the ashes. The option exists to keep them in an urn at home, scattered on the earth or out at sea or buried in the ground, and with time people are becoming more confident about disposal. When Kate was declared dead on admission to hospital after being run down by a car right outside her home, her parents were so shocked at the image of her broken body that they decided that fire was cleansing and opted for cremation. They're not sure whether or not it was a good idea. Her mother couldn't bear to part with the ashes. Initially they sat in an urn on top of the sideboard. When friends and family suggested that this was macabre, she put them on her dressing table. With hindsight she now reckons that she didn't really let go of Kate until they buried her ashes in the family plot in Gort some two years after her death.

HELP AGENCIES

Throughout Ireland there are several local set-ups to cater for the needs of the community. Information can be found in telephone directories, on the notice-boards at the back of churches; in health centres, doctors' surgeries etc.

AIDS ALLIANCE is the contact and national umbrella group for voluntary groups working with HIV positives and people with AIDS. Group headquarters and Dublin AIDS Alliance are at Avoca House, 189/193 Parnell Street, Dublin 1. Tel: 01-733799/01-733065/01-733480.

Cork AIDS Alliance, 16 Peter Street, Cork. Tel: 021-275837

Western AIDS Alliance, Ozman House, St Augustine Street, Galway. Tel: 091-66266

The following can be contacted through the AIDS Alliance offices:

CAIRDE – a confidential befriending service for people either directly or indirectly affected by the AIDS virus.

BODY POSITIVE – a self-support group offering emotional and practical support for people directly affected with AIDS.

WOMEN AND AIDS – a group that provides information and education to women either directly or indirectly affected by HIV or AIDS.

129

AIDS HELP LINE – a voluntary telephone helpline. Dublin, 01-724277; Cork, 021-276676; Galway, 091-66266.

CASA, the Caring and Sharing Association, is a voluntary group which befriends sick and disabled people. Over the past number of years the focus has been on taking mainly very sick and terminally-ill people to Lourdes. CASA has groups in Dublin, Cork, Antrim, Down, Kerry, Limerick, Longford and Tipperary. The Dublin contact is: Carmichael House, North Brunswick Street, Dublin 7, PO Box 1169, Tel: 01-725300/725370; and Cork: The Annex, Good Shepherd Convent, Sundays Well, Cork. Tel:021-342995/343040.

COPING is a voluntary organisation providing emotional support and practical advice for families caring at home for children with leucodystrophies and other rare progressive neurological disorders. COPING offers, where necessary, professional nursing care and provides specialist advice, support and encouragement for terminally-ill children and their families. The organisation provides a professional counselling service, encourages liaison between all those medically involved to ensure total patient care in the home. Information on assistance provided by local community care services is readily available. Where possible, COPING offers financial support for any necessary expenses required to be carried out which are outside the specific area of the Department of Health.

For further information, contact Rosaleen and Ken Corbet, 132 Glenageary Avenue, Glenageary, Co Dublin. Tel: 01- 285 6084

THE CYSTIC FIBROSIS ASSOCIATION OF IRELAND was founded in 1963. Its aims are to finance research to find a cure for CF and in the meantime to improve on current methods of treatment; to establish branches and groups nationwide to help and to advise parents with the everyday problems of caring for those affected by CF; to educate the public about the disease and through wider knowledge, to help to promote earlier diagnosis in young children. Contact The Cystic Fibrosis Association of Ireland, 24 Lr Rathmines Road, Dublin 6. Tel: 01-962433.

THE IRISH CANCER SOCIETY, founded in 1963 and financed by voluntary contributions, is the national charity dedicated to the control and eradication of cancer. As well as research and education, the Society is involved in patient care and support.

A free Home Care Service is available throughout the country to patients with cancer. Based in local hospitals or health centres, the nurses provided are specially trained in symptom control and patient/family counselling. The night nursing service operates nationwide. It provides a night nurse, free of charge, for up to five nights to families nursing a very ill cancer patient at home.

The Irish Cancer Society's support groups are based on recovered cancer patients working in a voluntary capacity to provide emotional support and practical advice to new patients and their families. Special support groups are:

REACH TO RECOVERY, for women before and after breast surgery

LARYNGECTOMY ASSOCIATION, for those who are about to have or have recently had surgery for throat cancer.

COLOSTOMY CARE ASSOCIATION, for those who are about to have or have recently had surgery for cancer of the colon or rectum.

HODGKINS UNITED GROUP (HUG), for people who have Hodgkins Disease or non-Hodgkins Lymphoma, and their families.

KIDS LIKE ME, for teenage cancer patients supported by the Irish Cancer Society, but organised out of Our Lady's Hospital for Sick Children, Crumlin, Dublin.

The Irish Cancer Society is at 5 Northumberland Road, Dublin 4. Tel: Dublin 01-681855; Cork 021-509759. For information on cancer and further details about the groups call freephone Cancer Helpline 1 800 200 300

THE IRISH MOTOR NEURON DISEASE ASSOCIATION was founded in 1985 by a small group of friends, relatives and carers of Motor Neuron Disease sufferers. The Association functions mainly as a support organisation for people who have MND, and their carers and families. This work entails home visiting, financial assistance for home nursing and supply of specialised equipment to patients. The Association also supports research into the causes and treatment of MND. Irish Motor Neuron Disease Association, Carmichael House, North Brunswick Street, Dublin 7, Tel: 01-730422.

ISIDA, The Irish Sudden Infant Death Association was founded in 1976 to offer support and information to families bereaved by Sudden Infant Death Syndrome, commonly known as cot death; to provide accurate and up-to-date information on cot death to health care and other concerned professionals, the media and the community in general; and to promote and support research into the causes and prevention of cot death.

ISIDA is a registered charity and a national organisation with members and branches throughout the country. It is affiliated to SIDS Family International, a worldwide federation of cot death parents' associations. It is currently funding several cot death research programmes, research grants being awarded on the recommendation of ISIDA's Scientific Advisory Committee.

A welcome innovation was the Book of Remembrance, to commemorate babies who had died cot deaths, which was launched at an interdenominational memorial service. The book records the names, ages and dates of birth and death of the babies together with a short message or inscription from each baby's parents.

The ISIDA National Office is located at Carmichael House, 4 North Brunswick Street, Dublin 7. ISIDA can also be contacted by post or by telephoning 01-747007, or fax 01-735737.

ISIDA provides the following services free of charge:
- A twenty-four hour telephone HELPLINE and information service at 01-747007
- A one-to-one or couple-to-couple befriending service
- Drop-in centres for bereaved families
- An information booklet on cot death and bereavement

- A twice-yearly newsletter and two annual seminars
- Community-based meetings
- An information service on cot death and its research for health care and other concerned professionals, the media and the general public
- Training of members to provide support and befriending services
- Posters, sponsorship cards and T-shirts for fundraising purposes.

THE NATIONAL REHABILITATION BOARD, 25 Clyde Road, Dublin 4, Tel: 01-684181, provides information on aids and equipment, on sources of supply and the cost of same.

THE NATIONAL SOCIAL SERVICES BOARD, 71 Lower Leeson Street, Dublin 2, Tel: 01-616422, Advice and a booklet, *Entitlements for the Disabled,* available free-of-charge. The NSSB has a directory of national voluntary organisations which is updated regularly.

The **SAMARITANS** are are on duty twenty-four hours a day, 365 days of the year, to befriend people who are anxious, depressed or suicidal. Their main objective is not so much to prevent suicide, but rather to prevent the isolation, loneliness, anxiety or despair that can lead to it. Their emphasis is on befriending and supporting people rather than solving problems and they accept the caller's own principles and beliefs by being non-judgemental and non-directive. The Samaritans work anonymously and guarantee absolute confidentiality and no interference. Contact can be made by phoning, writing or calling in person. Tel: Cork 021-271323; Dublin 01-727700; Ennis 065-29777; Galway 091-61222; Limerick 061-412111; Sligo 071-42011; Tralee 066-22566; Waterford 051-72114; Athlone 0902-73133

BIBLIOGRAPHY

The Ward Sister's Survival Guide, Austen Cornish Publishers, London, 1990.

The Staff Nurse's Survival Guide, Austen Cornish Publishers, London, 1990.

The Other Side of Surgery, Janet Gooch, Macmillan Press, London 1990.

Effective Communication(for the professional nurse), Austen Cornish Publishers, London 1990.

Hospice, The Living Idea, Cicely Saunders, Edward Arnold, a division of Hodder & Stoughton, London, 1981.

Sharing the Darkness, Sheila Cassidy, Darton, Longman & Todd, London, 1988.

Facing Death, Averil Stedeford, Heinemann Medical Books, Oxford, 1984.

On Death & Dying, Elisabeth Kübler-Ross, Tavistock Publications, London, 1970.

To Live Until We Say Goodbye, text by Elisabeth Kübler-Ross, photographs by Mal Warshaw, Prentice-Hall International Inc., USA, 1978.

Terminal Care at Home, edited by Roy Shilling, Oxford University Press, Oxford, 1988.

Suicide & Euthanasia, Historical and Contemporary Themes, edited by Baruch A. Brody, Kluwer Academic Publishers, Dordrecht/Boston/London, 1989.

Attempted Suicide, Keith Hawton, Jose Catalan, Oxford Medical Publications, 1987.

Suicide, Emile Durkheim, Routledge & Kegan Paul, London, 1987.

Dying with Love

Death without Dignity, edited by Nigel M. de S. Cameron, Rutherford House Books, Edinburgh, 1990.
Death, Dissection and the Destitute, Ruth Richardson, Routledge & Kegan Paul, London and New York, 1987.